# RIFLES

## OF THE WORLD

Produced by Copyright S.A.R.L., Paris, France
Photography by Matthieu Prier
Translated from the French by Charles Polley
in association with First Edition Translations Ltd, Cambridge, U.K.
Edited by David Gibbon

CHARTWELL BOOKS
A division of Book Sales, Inc.
POST OFFICE BOX 7100
114 Northfield Avenue
Edison, N.J. 08818-7100
CLB 3496
© 1994 this English language edition
CLB Publishing, Godalming, Surrey, U.K.
All rights reserved
Printed and bound in Spain by Graficas Estella
ISBN 1-55521-997-7

# RIFLES
## OF THE WORLD

Olivier Achard

CHARTWELL
BOOKS, INC.

# CONTENTS

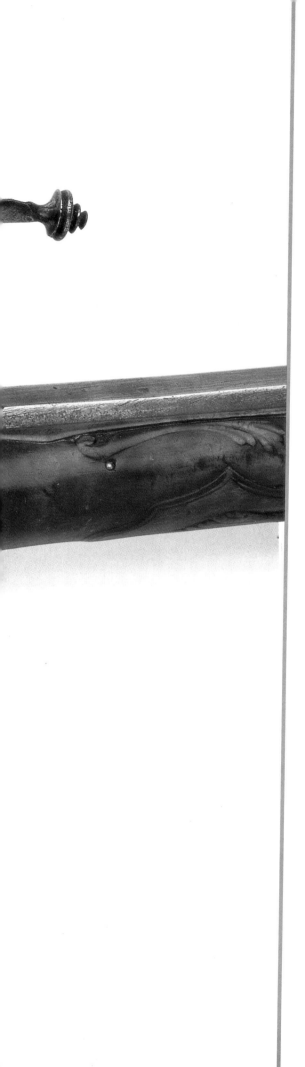

# A HISTORY OF THE LONG-BARRELED FIREARM

The invention of gunpowder caused the greatest upheaval in the history of mankind. The origin of the invention is shrouded in mystery. Some say it was invented by the Chinese, while others credit the Persians, the Greeks or the Arabs. According to another story, it was invented by a Franciscan monk named Berthold Schwarz, who was born in Germany between 1310 and 1330. Still others say it was in fact another monk, Roger Bacon (1214-1294), who was the real inventor of gunpowder. The theories are not fully convincing, though, and do not bear close investigation. It looks as though we must accept that the inventor's identity will never be known for sure. What we can be certain of is that when gunpowder appeared it revolutionized the art of warfare. Gunpowder was first applied to the creation of that famous artillery piece, the bombard, or mortar. The thickest walls offered very little resistance to the solid shot that was hurled from the bombard. Early versions fired stone shot, but very soon they were using projectiles made of low-grade castings also known as "pig iron."

The idea of being able to use portable artillery gained ground. The blunderbuss, a type of hand-held mortar, made its appearance. It was simply an iron tube, closed at one end, with a small touch hole in the closed end through which to light the gunpowder. It was a heavy, clumsy weapon with a fierce recoil, and clearly it needed refinement.

General view of a wheellock mechanism.
The wheellock was a great improvement over the other systems in existence at the time it was invented.

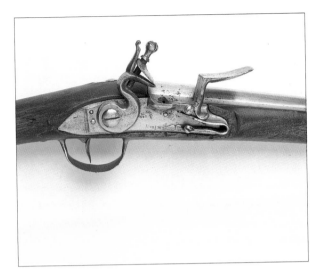

Detail of a flintlock.

A French gunsmith, Marin Le Bourgeoys, developed the most advanced flintlock mechanism ever made.

The barrel of the improved weapon was longer and had a smaller bore. It was attached to a piece of wood, which was a forerunner of the modern stock or rifle-butt. In later versions the touch hole was located on the right of the barrel rather than on top.

The blunderbuss gave way to the harquebus or arquebus. The derivation of the name is open to differing interpretations. The arquebus had a small dish, or "pan," around the touch hole, complete with a cover for protection from the weather. The weapon was fired using a smoldering match. However, the system was clumsy, and an improved mechanism made its appearance. This was the serpentine match holder, a small tube in the shape of an S which held the match. The serpentine was attached to the arquebus by a pivot. The shot was fired by simply swinging the serpentine into the pan so that the smoldering match set off the gunpowder. While reloading the weapon, the marksman would pull the serpentine back from the pan. With this system the shooter no longer ran the risk of burning his hand, as was often the case with the earlier mechanism.

The serpentine mechanism was improved in a number of minor ways. The swivel for the match holder was attached to a metal part known as a "lock," and the lock itself was attached to the wooden stock. Although the matchlock system had helped to make the arquebus easier to fire, there were still some disadvantages. The first was that the method did not work in rain or high winds. Another was that the shooter made an easy target at night because of the red glow from the match. These problems needed to be solved.

The next step was to fit the arquebus with a wheellock. The wheellock was a sort of rough disk fitted with a type of pawl known as a "dog head" or "cock." This was connected to the wheel by a spring. The cock was in fact hardly more than a metal rod with jaws at one end gripping a "fire-stone" of either genuine flint or iron pyrites. The shooter would wind the spring with a small key. Squeezing the trigger released the cock from the spring so that it struck the pan. The fire-stone would then produce a shower of sparks which lit the gunpowder and fired the shot. The biggest problem with the wheellock was its high cost, since it had to be made with such great accuracy. A simplified version of the wheellock gave rise to the flintlock.

Once the concept of striking flint against metal had found favor, gunsmiths tried simplifying the system in all sorts of ways. The Dutch developed a system known as the "rogue," or snaphaunce lock, while the Spanish developed the "brigand," or "miquelet." In 1610 a French gunsmith, Marin Le Bourgeoys, invented a mechanism that was felt to be the ultimate refinement of the flintlock. Rifles fitted with the new flintlock were taken up throughout Europe. The flintlock was certainly reliable, but still worked best only in good weather.

A Scottish Presbyterian minister, Alexander Forsyth, had noticed that if fulminate was exposed to flame or was given a sharp blow, it produced a flame of its own. He decided to apply his discovery to firearms. A fulminate percussion cap was placed over the touch hole. Removing the flint from the cock transformed it into a hammer which struck the fulminate cap. The cap burst into flame, lit the gunpowder and so fired the shot.

This discovery was a success. Attention swung away from the flintlock to the percussion lock, leading to the development of breech-loading weapons in preference to the muzzle-loading weapons of the past. Later, the idea of including the priming cap, gunpowder and bullet in a single wrapper gave rise to the modern cartridge. In this the shot is fired by striking the priming cap (a type of detonator) with a small metal rod called a firing-pin. The portable firearm had entered the modern era.

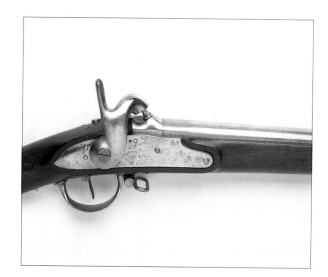

General view of a percussion lock.

13

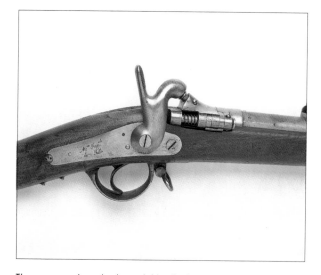

The percussion lock quickly led to the development of breech-loading weapons. Muzzle-loading weapons became obsolete.

# LONG GUNS: DEFINITIONS AND NAMING OF PARTS

The term "long gun" is clumsy, but it serves to distinguish weapons that are fired from the shoulder – such as arquebuses, muskets, rifles, shotguns and carbines – from a number of other categories of firearms such as side-arms (pistols or revolvers), machine-guns capable of fully automatic fire, and heavy guns or pieces of artillery which are not readily portable and which typically require more than one operator.

A long gun may be muzzle-loading or breech-loading, and if it is breech-loading it will be either a break-gun or a fixed barrel. It may also be smooth-bore or rifled; and, of course, it may be fired by percussion (all modern guns), by a flint-lock or wheel-lock, or by a match.

Muzzle-loading guns are simplest. The barrel is open at one end (the MUZZLE) and closed at the other (the BREECH). At the breech end, the propellant burns in the CHAMBER, which may be of the same diameter as the barrel or (in some old guns) of a smaller diameter. Beside the chamber is the TOUCH-HOLE (for match-fired guns, flint-locks and wheel-locks) or PERCUSSION NIPPLE (for cap-and-ball guns). Cartridge-firing guns will not have a touch-hole or percussion nipple. The CHARGE is tipped down the barrel, followed by the BALL which is seated with a RAMROD.

In the case of smooth-bore guns firing small shot, the barrel may be CHOKED or restricted at the muzzle; this allows a tighter grouping of shot at a distance, which increases the effective range of the gun. With small shot, two WADS are used: disks of felt, the first of which holds the charge in place, and the second of which retains the shot.

A break-gun is adequately described by its name, and is typified by the classic English side-by-side shotgun. A BREECH LOCK allows the break action, and fixes the barrels to the BLOCK by means of a BOLT which normally engages in the LUMP below the barrels: the barrels pivot around the CROSS-PIN. A RIB runs between the two barrels of a side-by-side gun, or along the top of an over-and-under gun, to aid sighting.

Fixed-barrel breech-loaders close the breech with a BOLT (which moves parallel with the barrel) or with a BLOCK which moves at right angles to it.

Percussion CARTRIDGES or the PERCUSSION CAPS in an older gun are detonated by the FIRING PIN or HAMMER; on a modern gun there may or may not be an external SPUR to allow the action to be cocked with the user's thumb. Guns with no external spur are known as HAMMERLESS. The SAFETY CATCH is a button or lever which blocks the action so that the gun cannot be fired accidentally: the TRIGGER GUARD around the TRIGGER performs a similar function, albeit less efficiently, and is omitted on some old weapons.

An AUTOMATIC EXTRACTOR removes spent cartridges; a plain extractor extracts both spent and unspent cartridges. An EJECTOR projects spent cartridges away from the gun.

The barrel is mounted on the STOCK, which rests against the shoulder (the BUTT) and the shooter's cheek (the COMB) and provides a grip for the hand which operates the TRIGGER; the FORE-END STOCK is steadied by the other hand.

Guns may be further classified according to the barrel length, the number of barrels – you will find more about multi-barreled guns on page 45 – and whether the barrels are smooth-bore (like a shotgun) or rifled.

In particular, the CARBINE is today a short-barreled version of the military rifle, where it exists at all; the reduction in length is solely to make it handier and more portable, as in the Lee-Enfield "Jungle Carbine" which is easier to carry through dense undergrowth. For obvious reasons, cavalry used to be heavy users of carbines, which are easier to carry, load and fire on horseback. To some extent, the MUSKETOON is a form of carbine, though the word can also be synonymous with BLUNDERBUSS, which is a short-barreled, flared-mouth gun with a smooth bore: the idea of the latter was to produce a gun which was effective only at short range, but which could do tremendous execution at up to five yards or so. The flared mouth of the blunderbuss was meant to act in exactly the opposite way to a choke, by spreading the shot rather than bunching it.

---

In French and some other European languages, the term "carbine" ("carabine" in French) is however also used for very high-powered rifles, typically used for shooting big game. The chambers are tested to very much higher pressures than normal guns, often three times as high, and huge bullets (often 0.5 inches in diameter, 12.7mm, or bigger) can be fired at the very high velocities which are required to stop a charging rhinoceros or a leaping lion. In English, these are more often known as "express rifles," though strictly this refers to double-barreled rifles designed for big game: the second barrel provides a reserve of stopping power in case the target is not convinced by the first barrel. Shooting these monster guns requires considerable practice, as the recoil is tremendous.

The sights on these big "carbines" are typically rather more highly developed than those on other sporting guns, being rather closer to those found on military weapons.

Carbines have metal sighting systems: an OPTICAL SIGHT or a SIGHTING NOTCH, either of which may be mounted on a REARSIGHT LEAF, and a FRONTSIGHT which may be adjustable and is sometimes protected by a FRONTSIGHT HOUSING.

"Battue" carbines have a wide, prominent, clearly defined "battue" rib which does not reach to the end of the barrel.

A carbine can be fitted with a TELESCOPIC SIGHT.

The forepart of a carbine generally has a wooden grip called a FOREND or FOREGRIP, which may be short or long. A long forend reaching to the end of the barrel is called a STUTZEN.

Carbines sometimes have a double trigger. The first of these is the SET TRIGGER or STECHER, for adjusting the force of the shot discharged by the second trigger.

Left to right: a pin-fire cartridge, three center-fire cartridges for rifle-bore weapons, and a paper cartridge.

A center-fire cartridge for smooth-bore weapons (16 caliber), two center-fire cartridges for rifle-bore weapons (300 W. and 30-30 caliber), and a rimfire cartridge (22 boscage caliber).

Basic components of a center-fire cartridge for smooth-bore rifles.

Basic components of a center-fire cartridge for rifle-bore weapons.

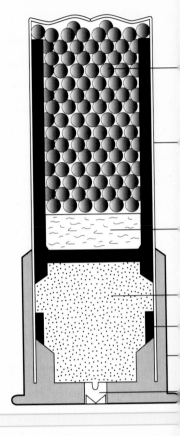
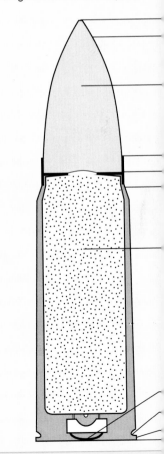

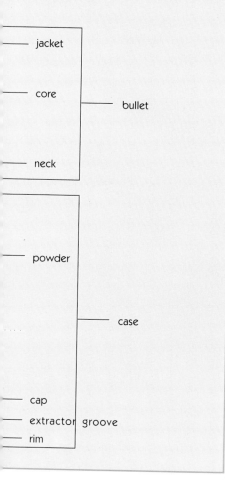

lead shot

case

wad (shock absorbent material)

powder

case

brass head or case-head

primer

jacket

core

neck

bullet

powder

case

cap

extractor groove

rim

# AMMUNITION

Ammunition is an inseparable part of the firearm itself.

### A BRIEF HISTORY OF AMMUNITION

Shooters originally loaded their weapons at the muzzle, first putting in black powder and then a lead ball. This was a very slow procedure, and someone had the idea of wrapping the gunpowder and ball in one piece of paper. It then became a simple matter to include the primer in the paper cartridge along with the powder and ball. With this method, the weapon could be loaded at the breech. Several different ammunition systems made their appearance: the needle cartridge, the rimfire cartridge, the pin-fire cartridge and eventually the center-fire cartridge.

### DESCRIBING AMMUNITION

Ammunition is described mainly in terms of the caliber of the weapon it is intended to fit.

### AMMUNITION FOR SMOOTH-BORE GUNS

The number refers to the number of spherical balls which would fit exactly into the bore in question and which can be cast from one pound (454 grammes) of lead: thus, 12 balls from a 12-bore would weigh one pound, 20 balls from a 20-bore, and so forth. If there is a second number, for example 12/76, it refers to the length of the cartridge in millimetres; the 76mm 12-bore cartridge is also known as the Magnum 12.

### AMMUNITION FOR RIFLED GUNS

The number here can refer to the actual diameter of the ammunition; to the distance between the bottoms of two opposite grooves in the rifling; to the distance across the lands between the rifling, plus twice the depth of one rifling groove (for those guns where the grooves are not opposite one another); or to the distance between the lands. What is more, it may be in millimetres or inches, and it may be actual or nominal. Examples include 6.5mm, 7.62mm, .22 (inch), .303 (inch).

And this is only the first number. The second number in most modern arms refers to the length of the case in millimetres, as in 7.62 x 51mm (which is also a .308 Winchester in a two-inch case), but it can also refer to quite a variety of other things. For example, 45-75 refers to a .45 inch bullet propelled by 75 grains of powder, while 30-06 refers to a .30 caliber adopted in 1906. Then there are those cases where the cartridge is "necked" so that a bullet of one diameter is seated in a cartridge of another. This is the way that "wildcat" (non-standard) cartridges are often designated. Finally, there may be a letter.

In the metric system the second figure gives the length of the cartridge case in millimeters. 7.62 x 51mm means a 7.62mm caliber on a 51mm cartridge case. In the Anglo-American system, the first number may be followed by a dash, for example: 45-75 or 30-06. The first figure, 45, refers to the caliber, and the second, 75, to the quantity of gunpowder expressed in grains. For the 30-06, 30 defines the caliber, as before, but 06 is the year it was adopted (1906). An oblique stroke or dash (6/222 or 6mm-222 Remington) means the ammunition is a 6mm caliber bullet on a 222 caliber cartridge case. In the metric system, if a number is followed by a letter as in 9.3 x 74 R, the R stands for Rand, meaning the cartridge case has a rim rather than a neck. When the American system uses a letter, it usually means the name of the person or firm that created the ammunition. R. means Remington and W. means Winchester. This only applies to ammunition created before 1970. The metric system applies from then on.

A period of French history laden with tragedy is depicted on this remarkable rifle made for the famous contemporary gunsmith, Jacky Brusson. The portraits of Louis XVI and Marie-Antoinette on the shells, the scenes of the flight to Varennes and the death of the martyr king, together with the fleurs-de-lys,

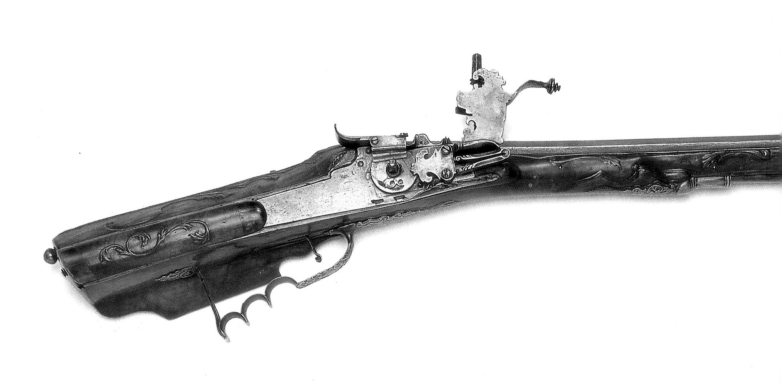

# HISTORICAL WEAPONS

took the engraver Freycon seven hundred hours to complete. Georges Grangier was entrusted with making this side-by-side. It has a Holland & Holland lock and a patented Aiglon closure developed in 1913 by Aimé Coeur Tyrod, whose successor Guichard won a gold medal in Paris in 1937.

Antique weapons are generally the most prized by collectors, but the definition of "antique" varies from place to place, and it is impossible to give reliable guidelines; you will have to check with your local police (or better still, with your local gun club) to see what the rules are.

An antique firearm is not, as some might think, a few bits of wood and metal simply thrown together. An antique firearm is a fragment of our cultural and historical heritage. First and foremost it bears witness to history, a history filled with conquests, victories and defeats, joys and tears.

An arms collector is not just interested in weapons for their own sake, but is above all a devotee of history. Buying an antique weapon is not like buying a tin of beans. The antique weapons enthusiast must know enough not to be "sold a pup," which sadly happens now and then.

Purchasing a firearm is the culmination of a long process of research through books and archives, museums and specialist dealers, as well as salesrooms.

But what a feeling of delight when the quarry you have been stalking for so long is at last within your reach!

Top left: German wheellock carbine dated 1595.
Bottom left: Small Austrian wheellock carbine dating from the 17th century.

Infantry rifle of 1728 type
Caliber: 17.5mm
Weight: 4.1kg (9 lb)
Length overall: 1590mm (62.5 in)

Imperial Guard light-infantry rifle of 1777 type
Caliber: 17.5mm
Weight: 4.6kg (10 lb)
Length overall: 1520mm (60 in)

Model T40 infantry rifle of 1822 type
Caliber: 18mm
Weight: 4.2kg (9 lb 4 oz)
Length overall: 1470mm (58 in)

French infantry rifle of the 1867 "Snuff-box" type
Caliber: 17.8mm
Weight: 4.45kg (9 lb 13 oz)
Length overall: 1420mm (56 in)

Lock finely marked "Jourjon" and stamped Saint-Etienne. Barrel with many fine punch marks on the left side. Fine "cow's hoof" stock. Rare.

This rifle was also issued to the horse grenadiers, the foot artillery and the engineers. Lock finely marked from Versailles and stamped Niçaise. All fittings bronze with a rather stronger trigger guard than those used by other troops, and butt-plate return with floral embellishment. Breech tail clearly marked M 1777. Gray metal, slight pitting here and there, joined foregrip. Extremely rare.

# THE FRENCH INFANTRY RIFLE

Percussion conversion of the system developed by Captain Arcellin (first percussion conversion system). Brightly polished metal. Barrel with good caliber marking, breech tail with nice year mark. Lock bearing a light mark of the Manufacture Royale de Tulle. Fine wood with the badge of the Saint-Etienne repair shop 1865. Used as a reserve weapon at the end of the French Second Empire. A firearm of great historical significance.

Lock finely marked "Manufacture Impériale de Tulle," barrel showing numerous inspection stamps. Stock stamped "October 1866." Manufactured in that year but immediately converted to the "snuff-box" type, which explains its exceptional state of preservation. Almost as if it had never been fired.

Percussion target rifle
Caliber: 15mm
Overall length: 1410mm (55.5 in)

1819 pattern Hall US Breech-Loading (1838)
Caliber: 52mm rifled barrel
Overall length: 1340mm (52.75 in)

24

Russian sharpshooter's Stutzen carbine,
1843 type
Overall length: 1180mm (46.5 in)

Belgian Tersen carbine of 1848/68
Caliber: 11mm
Length: 1280mm (50 in)

Rifle signed "Lanavit," listed as a gunsmith in Senlis (France) in 1855. Excellent barrel with hair-line rifling. Gray metal, adjustable rearsight, precision sighting notch. Pistol grip stock in perfect condition, foregrip extends fully to muzzle, no cleaning rod holder. Fish-tail butt plate.

2nd production flintlock rifle. Metal excellent for a firearm of this type, original sheen with a very few small spots of surface oxidation. Interior mirror-finish in places, with excellent rifling. Markings clearly readable. Woodwork with nice patina on original grain. The cleaning rod is the only non-original item. 19,680 Hall rifles were manufactured from 1817 to 1840. These flintlocks were taken up by the US Army in 1819.

# AN ASSORTMENT OF ARMS

Made in Liège by J.-P. Malherbe, this rifle has a finely marked lock, together with a registration mark and double-headed eagle stamp on the butt-plate return. Thumb-rest bears the cipher of Czar Nicholas I. Damascus barrel has lost its color, other metal components in good condition. Patina on stock with excellent stampings, signs of original varnish. Barrel design influenced by the Brunswick military rifle from England, with two deep rifling grooves.

Derived from a conversion of the 1848 flintlock rifle. One-piece stock and woodwork, new barrel attached to the foregrip by bands. Ramrod below the barrel. Lock on the right due to the conversion from flint to percussion. Frame, lock and breech very fine, patina on steel. Barrel 70 percent bronzed. Mirror-bright inside, with superb rifling. Good punch-markings. Woodwork has nice patina.

Double rifle of the Corsican light infantry
Caliber: 17.5mm
Weight: 4.5kg (9 lb 14 oz)
Overall length: 1210mm (48 in)

Plains rifle WM Read, Boston
Caliber: 9.5mm
Overall length: 1160mm (45.6 in)
Round percussion barrel 787mm long (31 in)

Sharps sporting rifle 1853 model
Caliber: 45 for "paper" cartridges
Weight: 3.6kg (7 lb 15 oz)
Length of octagonal percussion barrel: 660mm (26 in)
Overall length: 1065mm (42 in)

Dreyse 1857 pattern Prussian cavalry carbine
Overall length: 805mm (31.5 in)
Barrel length: 370mm (14.5 in)

Pattern of 1850. Made at Saint-Etienne in very limited numbers. Damascus barrel in a lightish shade. Locks finely marked, polished white. The characteristically shaped dog-heads still have their marbling. Handsomely striped stock. Complete with ramrod. Very rare piece.

Patches of chocolate metal on 255mm (10 in) of the heavy barrel. The inside is mirror-bright in places, very fine, with superb rifling and just a touch of oxidation. Fore-plate engraved with game-birds and flowers. Fine marking. Normal rearsight and adjustable peephole. Woodwork sound and nicely patinated, brass patchbox. Rare weapon in this condition and character. Used in the Robert Redford film *Jeremiah Johnson*.

This is the Sharps "Buffalo" with double Stecher trigger. Very impressive barrel of 25mm (1 in) cross-section at the muzzle. Gray steel frame with some remaining signs of oxidation. The highly smooth barrel has been re-blued some time ago, and is bright in parts. Patina on stock and forend. Joins at the stock grip. Patchbox, iron butt plate. Nickel silver ferrule on foregrip. Rare.

Very short firearm. Metal cleaned, still showing a few signs of elephant skin tarnish. Some mirror brightness on the inside with a touch of oxidation, superb rifling. Readable markings. Fine stampings. Very sound woodwork and just a trace of handling.

# SPORTING RIFLES

Traditionally, the right to bear arms was the mark of a free man. Today, those who hunt with the gun are carrying on this proud tradition.

The first twin-barreled fowling pieces appeared as early as the 16th century. Welding techniques developed in the 18th century meant that double-barreled rifles could then be mass-produced. The beginnings of the true revolution in firing actions came about with the appearance of the Pottet center-fire cartridge and the pin-fire cartridge developed by Casimir Lefaucheux.

Between 1852 and 1880, mechanical inventions came thick and fast, and by the start of the 20th century there was the widest choice of sporting rifles that had ever been available. Whereas military circles tend to narrow the variety of their firearms down to a single, widely used weapon, sporting rifles keep all their special characteristics. There is a different kind of sporting rifle for almost every type of game hunted. To put it mildly, the choice of weapons facing the enthusiast is more than adequate.

There are two main categories of sporting gun: the shotgun and the rifle. Shotguns have one or more smooth barrels, and rifles have one or more rifled barrels. There is also a third category, the combination weapon with a mixture of smooth and rifled barrels. Some combination weapons are thought of as rifles and others as shotguns. At the risk of shocking the purist, we shall put them in a third group of their own.

Probably the most widespread type of sporting long gun is the shotgun, a smooth-bore weapon used almost exclusively for small game. In most of the more populous and advanced countries of the world, though not in the United States, hunting larger game is a thing of the past: there is not enough game left, and the danger of accidentally shooting other people is adjudged too great.

Sporting rifles can be divided into four groups, or in fact five if you include pump-action guns, though many consider them to be more suitable for personal defense than hunting. The traditional sporting weapon is the double-barreled, side-by-side hinged shotgun. This very elegant gun is the most widely used type of sporting rifle. There is also the double-barreled over-and-under. In

**Merkel type 117**
Caliber: 20/70
Weight: 2.8kg (6 lb 3 oz)
Overall length: 1140mm (45 in)
Barrel length: 710mm (28 in)

Very elegant de luxe weapon with direct firing-pin action, side-mounted cocking indicator, Holland & Holland ejector, double trigger. English-style walnut stock. Arabesque chasing with decorated edge-strip and screws.

**Beretta 626 E**
Caliber: 12/70
Weight: 3 kg (6 lb 10 oz)
Overall length: 1140mm (45 in)
Barrel length: 710mm (28 in)

This magnificent side-by-side has a double trigger and top safety catch. English-style checkered walnut stock and forend. Arabesque chasing.

# SHOTGUNS

the last couple of decades the over-and-under has become very popular because it costs less. Technically speaking, it is actually a lot easier to manufacture an over-and-under than a side-by-side. In third place and losing ground rapidly is the single-shot sporting rifle. The main disadvantage of this weapon is that it does not give you a second shot. Because it is lighter it tends to be a favorite with beginners. Lastly there are the automatics, or rather the semi-automatics. These are not very popular with hunting and rough-shooting enthusiasts, who feel they can cause accidents. Not only that, but the environmentally aware gun owner also knows it is not acceptable to leave spent cartridge cases lying around. The problem is, it takes longer to find every spent cartridge from an automatic than from other kinds of gun.

**Browning 325 sporting rifle**
Caliber: 12/70
Weight: 3.3kg (7 lb 4 oz)
Overall length: 1150mm (45 in)
Barrel length: 710mm (28 in)

Very well made firearm. Forged steel one-piece drop-down with antique silver finish. Gold-plated adjustable, single selective trigger. Walnut woodwork with checkering on both the pistol grip and the "tulip" forend.

**Beretta 686 ultra light**
Caliber: 12/70
Weight: 2.6kg (5 lb 12 oz)
Overall length: 1075mm (42 in)
Barrel length: 710mm (28 in)

Lightened version of the 686 with light-alloy black hinge. Special molybdenum chrome-nickel steel barrels, chromed interior. Automatic ejectors, ventilated rib and short side ribs. Being so light, this gun "kicks" a lot. It is wise to fit a rubber butt plate.

# SHOTGUNS
### SIDE-BY-SIDE
### OVER-AND-UNDERS

**Ferlib FV, Holland & Holland lock**
Caliber: 12/70

This superb gun is from the Italian firm Ferlib. Founded in 1952, Ferlib specializes in side-by-sides with H & H or Anson & Deeley de luxe locks.

**Piotti, King No 2**
Caliber: 12/70
Weight: 3.06kg (6 lb 12 oz)

This remarkable firearm has great charms for all fine weapon enthusiasts. Detachable locks and ejectors. Fully engraved drop-down plate. Burr walnut stock.

Manufrance Simplex rifle
Caliber: 12/70

Weight: 2.85kg (6 lb 4 oz)
Overall length: 1210mm (48 in)
Barrel length: 800mm (31 in)

Harrington & Richardson "Turkey Mag" rifle
Caliber: 12/76
Weight: 2.37kg (5 lb 3 oz)
Overall length: 1020mm (40 in)
Barrel length: 560mm (22 in)

Beretta A 304
Caliber: 12/70

Weight: 2.98kg (6 lb 9 oz)
3 shot
Overall length: 1200mm (47 in)
Barrel length: 710mm (28 in)

Verney Carron, Luxor Slug
3 shot (5 to order)
Caliber: 12/70
Weight: 3kg (6 lb 9 oz)
Barrel length: 610mm (24 in)

Rifle produced by the famous French firm of Manufrance in Saint-Etienne. Hinged barrel. This gun is tough enough to withstand just about anything.

Simple, very rugged weapon, ideal for the beginner. Camouflaged in "Mossy Oak." Powerful automatic ejector.

## SHOTGUNS
### SINGLE-SHOTS
### AUTOMATICS

Semi-automatic rifle operated by gas blowback. Extremely light. Engraved special alloy breech casing. Available with fixed or removable chokes.

Cold-forged, "super diamond" chrome-molybdenum steel barrel. Light, high-strength alloy breech casing. Double safety. Rearsight adjustable for height and direction, raked frontsight. Designed for precision shooting, can also be used for rough shooting.

Blaser K 77 Luxe carbine with 6x62
Frères ammunition
5th category weapon
Caliber: 6x62 R Frères
Weight: 2.7kg (5 lb 15 oz)
Overall length: 1300mm (51 in)
Barrel length: 600mm (24 in)

Rifles have one or more rifled gun barrels. They are more suitable for hunting larger game animals. Rifles can be divided into the same categories as shotguns, though it should be noted that a rifle with more than one barrel is often called an "express." People therefore sometimes talk of a side-by-side express or an over-and-under express. The name "express" was actually used to describe rifles made by Purdey (the "express trains" of the gun world). The name was taken up again by cartridge manufacturers Eley and Kinoch to designate ammunition like the 600 Nitro-express, intended for use against large game animals. "Express" later became the popular name for a double-barreled rifle.

# CARBINES
## SINGLE-SHOTS
## AUTOMATICS

Side-by-side or over-and-under expresses are very expensive because they are difficult to manufacture. The highly trained craftsmen who make them are uniquely qualified to solve the problems that arise from convergence of the barrels. Bolt-action weapons, also called repeaters, are simpler to make than expresses as well as being very rugged, and form the most popular category of rifle. Single-shot hinged rifles are usually luxury items for hunters who believe in killing with the first shot or letting the game escape. The final category covers semi-automatics. Their only advantage is their rapid fire capability.

Hinged single-shot rifle of great class. The Blaser K 77 is noted for its great lightness and superb handling characteristics. Blaser arms are all designed on the principle that they can be carried uncocked but loaded, and cocked silently by just pushing the safety button forward. On this de luxe version, the drop-down plate is fully engraved with animal scenes. The woodwork is in specially selected burr walnut.

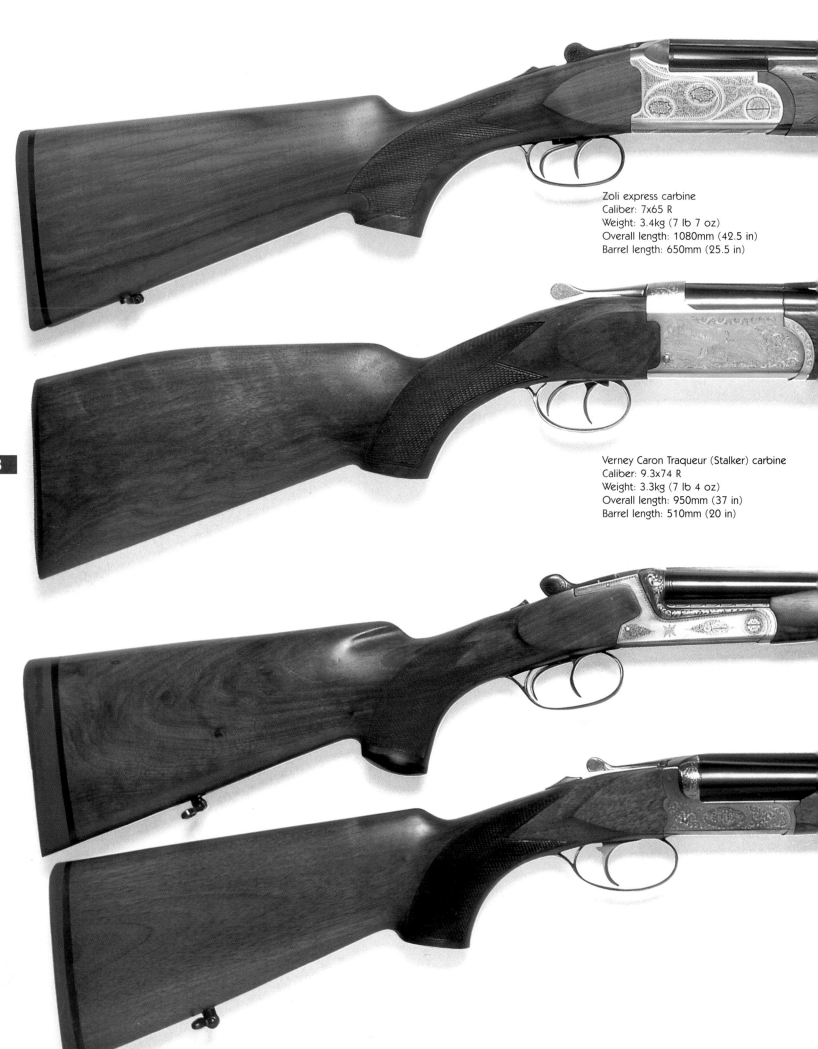

Zoli express carbine
Caliber: 7x65 R
Weight: 3.4kg (7 lb 7 oz)
Overall length: 1080mm (42.5 in)
Barrel length: 650mm (25.5 in)

Verney Caron Traqueur (Stalker) carbine
Caliber: 9.3x74 R
Weight: 3.3kg (7 lb 4 oz)
Overall length: 950mm (37 in)
Barrel length: 510mm (20 in)

Firearm by the famous Italian gunsmith Zoli, whose forebears have been making arms since the early 15th century. Special steel barrel, full rib with rearsight. Purdey type locking. Double Stecher trigger. Steel hinge with antique silver finish and hunting scenes engraved in relief. Oiled walnut stock with rubber heel.

Excellent quality weapon with direct center-fire percussion to prevent any risk of misfire. First-grade steel reinforced drop-down. The "battue" rib can be adjusted for height and comes with a machined mount for a telescopic sight. Double trigger. Curved walnut "hog's back" stock with Monte Carlo type cheekpiece and pistol grip. Checkered by hand.

**F.W. Heym, Model 88B express**
Caliber: 7x65 R
Weight: 3.6kg (7 lb 15 oz)
Overall length: 1060mm (41.5 in)
Barrel length: 635mm (25 in)

Two-shot over-and-under with drop-down barrels. Steel hinge action uses the Anson system, modified with double locking, Greener cross locking, button safety. Forward set trigger. Barrel in cold-forged Krupp special steel. Handsome walnut stock.

**Chapuis express, Chambord model**
Caliber: 9.3x74 R
Weight: 3.25kg (7 lb 2 oz)
Overall length: 1040mm (41 in)
Barrel length: 600mm (24 in)

Manufactured by this famous Saint-Etienne firm. Special steel barrel, "battue" rib and rearsight with patented luminous cross-hairs, adjustable frontsight. Accurate and easy to handle. Walnut stock without cheekpiece but with pistol grip, "tulip" forend, English-style heel and checkering by hand. English chasing with floral sprays, antique silver finish.

Kipplauf Borovnik rifle with
Habicht 2.2-9x42 R4 telescopic sight
Caliber: 6.5x65 R
Weight with optical sight:
    3.36kg (7 lb 6 oz)

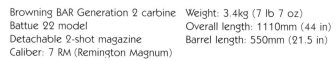

Browning BAR Generation 2 carbine    Weight: 3.4kg (7 lb 7 oz)
Battue 22 model                      Overall length: 1110mm (44 in)
Detachable 2-shot magazine           Barrel length: 550mm (21.5 in)
Caliber: 7 RM (Remington Magnum)

Remington model 7400 carbine         Weight: 3.4kg (7 lb 7 oz)
Detachable 2-shot magazine           Overall length: 1067mm (42 in)
Caliber: 280 Remington               Barrel length: 559mm (22 in)

Kipplauf Scheiring rifle
Caliber: 6x62 Frères
Weight: 2.78kg (6 lb 2 oz)

Carbine with opening and locking lever under the trigger guard. This arrangement is very safe because the gun cannot be fired unless the lever is completely closed. Attractive, Bavarian style stock in burr walnut with handsomely engraved buffalo horn forend.

Luxury carbine with octagonal barrel and Blitz mechanism. Narrow, flat drop-down. Burr walnut stock with forend and pistol grip by Kaisergriff with buffalo horn shape. Bavarian-style cheekpiece and decorated pistol grip. Engraved hunting scene ornamentation.

## CARBINES
### SINGLE-SHOTS
### SEMI-AUTOMATICS

Famous semi-automatic rifle operated by gas blowback. Seven-pin rotary locking system, gas take-up adjustment screw. Fitted with a "battue" rib and red translucent frontsight for a quick aim and instinctive shot. Mounting for optical sight. Mechanical push-button safety behind trigger. Matt varnished walnut stock.

Semi-automatic rifle operated by gas blowback. Adjustable rearsight. Monte Carlo type stock. Very accurate rifle.

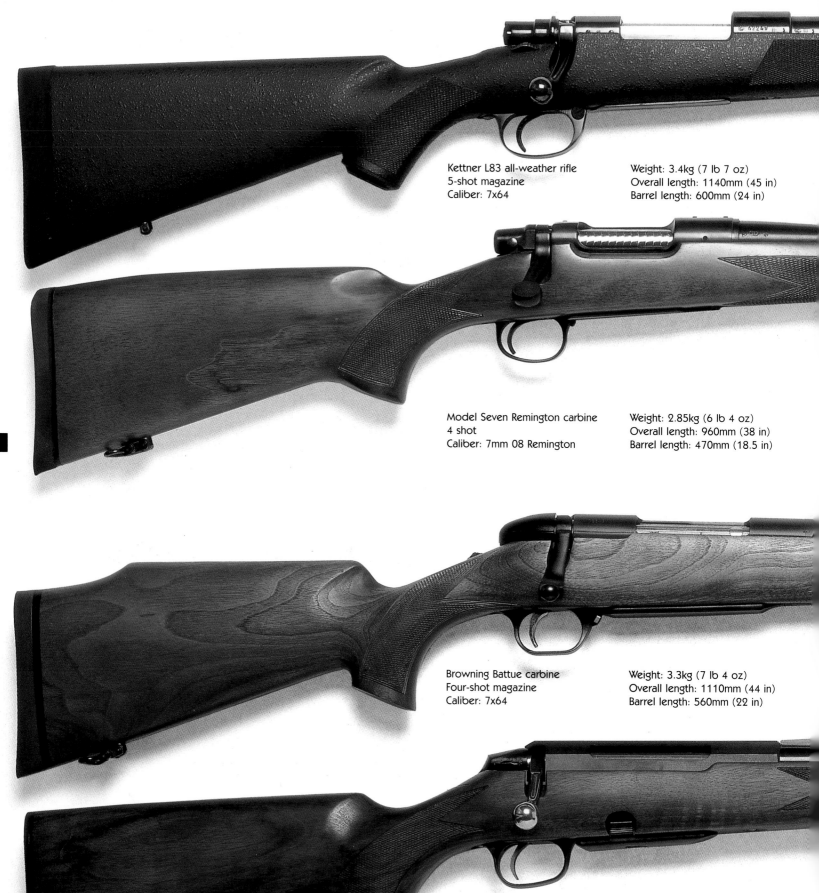

Kettner L83 all-weather rifle
5-shot magazine
Caliber: 7x64

Weight: 3.4kg (7 lb 7 oz)
Overall length: 1140mm (45 in)
Barrel length: 600mm (24 in)

Model Seven Remington carbine
4 shot
Caliber: 7mm 08 Remington

Weight: 2.85kg (6 lb 4 oz)
Overall length: 960mm (38 in)
Barrel length: 470mm (18.5 in)

Browning Battue carbine
Four-shot magazine
Caliber: 7x64

Weight: 3.3kg (7 lb 4 oz)
Overall length: 1110mm (44 in)
Barrel length: 560mm (22 in)

Tikka Model 690 carbine
Three-shot magazine
Caliber: 9.3x62

Weight: 3.2kg (7 lb 1oz)
Overall length: 1040mm (41 in)
Barrel length: 520mm (21 in)

All-weather carbine with Zastava breech and barrel, mounted on a synthetic, shock-resistant, unbreakable stock. Direct-action trigger. Detachable band swivel.

Very compact carbine, short breech, direct fire, available with Kevlar-reinforced glass fiber stock.

# CARBINES
## BOLT-ACTION RIFLES

Well-made rifle. High-quality walnut woodwork with tulip-style foregrip. Pistol grip with top safety, battue rib. Other versions available: European, Stalker, Stalker Magnum and Battue Magnum.

Highly accurate rifle of great class, with suspended barrel, adjustable battue rib and mounting for optical sight. Thoroughly reliable.

Koschat Bockdrilling with
Zeiss Diavari Z 1.5-6x42 optical sight
Caliber: 7x65 R-5.6x50-20/76
Weight (without optical sight): 4kg (8 lb 13 oz)
Barrel length: 610mm (24 in)

Borovnik Express-drilling with
S & Bender 1 1/4 telescopic sight
4x20 R4
Caliber: 9.3x74 R-20/76
Weight (without optical sight): 3.2kg (7 lb 1 oz)
Barrel length: 600mm (24 in)

Combination weapons are intended to cater for different types of hunting. They have a combination of smooth-bore and rifled barrels. Combination guns are usually built by craftsmen, which explains their high price. This type of gun is widely used in Germany and Austria.

The TRIPLE-BARRELED EXPRESS has two rifled barrels and one smooth-bore. This weapon is designed for hunting large game, but can also be used for small ground game.

The BERGSTUTZEN is a carbine used for hunting in the mountains. Bergstutzens have two barrels of different caliber. These may be side-by-side or over-and-under.

MIXED guns have one smooth-bore and one rifled barrel which may be side-by-side or over-and-under. These guns can be used for rough shooting or stalking big game.

The TRIPLE-BARREL is an all-purpose firearm with two smooth-bore barrels and one rifled barrel. The smooth barrels are usually side-by-side, with the rifled barrel above or below the other two. In rare examples the three barrels may be placed over-and-under.

The BOCKDRILLING is designed for use at close quarters. This is another triple-barreled weapon, this time

The two rifled barrels (caliber 9.3x74 R) are placed side-by-side. The smooth-bore barrel (caliber 20/76) is below. The barrels are Super Blitz steel, which is highly resistant to pressure so that barrel thickness and weapon weight can be reduced. The Bavarian-style stock is made of 5/6 walnut. Engraved with a hunting scene.

# COMBINATION WEAPONS

with one smooth-bore barrel and two rifled barrels of different caliber. They are usually over-and under. In some cases one barrel is slightly offset from the others. VIERLINGS have four barrels. Two are smooth-bored and of the same caliber. The other two are rifled barrels of different caliber. They are used like a standard triple-barrel but give a choice of the most suitable caliber for the game concerned.

The VIERLING EXPRESS is another four-barreled gun. In this case three of its barrels are rifled, two being of the same caliber. The fourth barrel is smooth-bored. As a general rule the two rifled barrels of the same caliber are side-by-side. The smooth-bore barrel is underneath and the smallbore rifled barrel is on top.

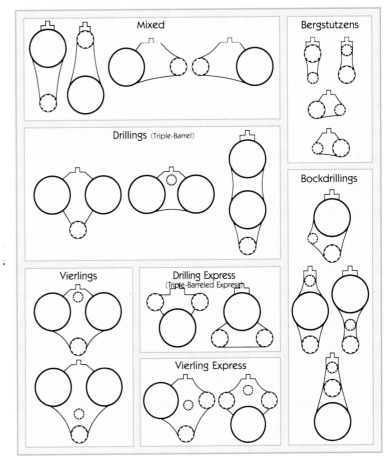

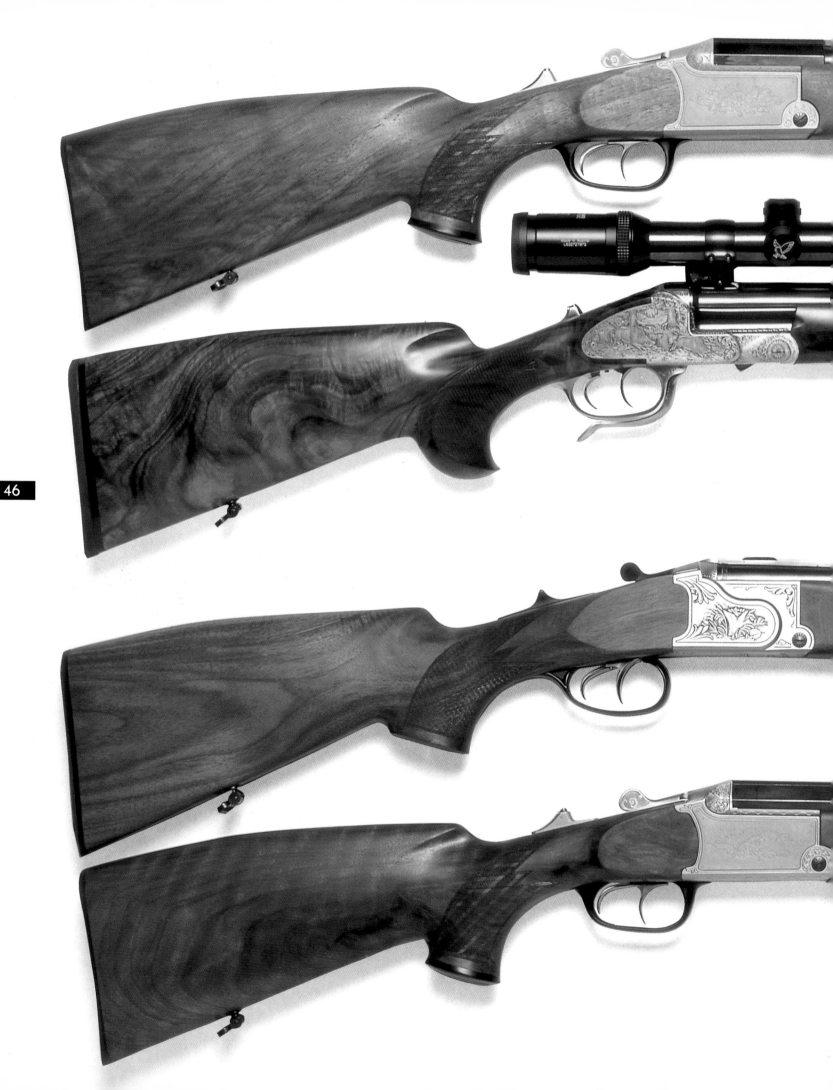

**Blaser model 700/88 combination rifle**
Caliber: 12/70-7x65 R
Weight: 2.8kg (6 lb 3 oz)
Overall length: 1030mm (40.5 in)
Barrel length: 600mm (24 in)

The Blaser 700/88 compound has been in production for around 30 years. It has undergone continuous development throughout that time. This weapon is among the finest in a combination rifle. The upper barrel is the smooth-bore (12/70) and the lower one is rifled (7x65 R). Fitted with the Blaser SLK system and adjustable triggers.

**Scheiring Dusel Bergstutzen with Habicht 2.2-9x42 4-cross-hair telescopic sight**
Caliber: 7mm Remington Magnum-5.6x50 R
Weight: 3.66kg (8 lb 1 oz)
Overall length: 1025mm (40 in)
Barrel length: 600mm (24 in)

Light and very manageable weapon well suited to hunting in the mountains.

# CARBINES
## COMBINATION WEAPONS

**Krieghoff Ultra 12**
Caliber: 12/70-9.3x74 R
Weight: 2.8kg (6 lb 3 oz)
Overall length: 1040mm (41 in)
Barrel length: 635mm (25 in)

Finest quality mixed rifle, double percussion system, ventilated rib, optical sight mounting. Engraved, antique silver finish drop-down.

**Blaser two-caliber 750/88, over-and-under Bergstutzen**
Caliber: 7x65 R-5.6x50 R Magnum
Weight: 3.1kg (6 lb 13 oz)
Overall length: 1030mm (40.5 in)
Barrel length: 600mm (24 in)

Mountain hunting weapon (Bergstutzen) for the ball ammunition specialist. This rifle has two barrels, each of a different caliber. The upper barrel receives 5.6x50 R magnum. The lower takes 7x65 R. The front trigger fires the large barrel. The rear trigger controls the smallbore barrel.

# HOBBY RIFLES

In reality or in dreams, weapons have held a certain fascination for most of us since the dawn of history. A citizen or freeman was at one time someone who had the right to bear arms.

In today's automated, standardized society, dominated as we are by market forces and the implacable laws of economics, our dreams are intimately linked through novels, the cinema or television to the ownership or use of weapons. With our fascination for weaponry we can instinctively use hobby shooting, target shooting or competition shooting as a means of attaining complete self-mastery.

Chief Commissioner Raymond Sasia, former Director of the French National Police Center for Weapons Training, wrote in his book *Le Tir Rapide* (Quick Shooting): "Shooting is a school in its own right, one in which we never cease to learn. When we practise a movement, our concern is not just for the method but also to ensure that the inner meaning, that is to say the spirit, is preserved. It is not about wounding or killing, but about going beyond our own limits, combating fatigue, heaviness, disorder, superficiality and the easy way out in our search for accuracy."

Hobby guns, sometimes called garden guns, are an unpretentious class of weapon, and particularly useful for training beginners. Within the reach of most budgets, they are easy to maintain and use. They bring friends together for some pleasant, non-competitive shooting, just for the fun of it.

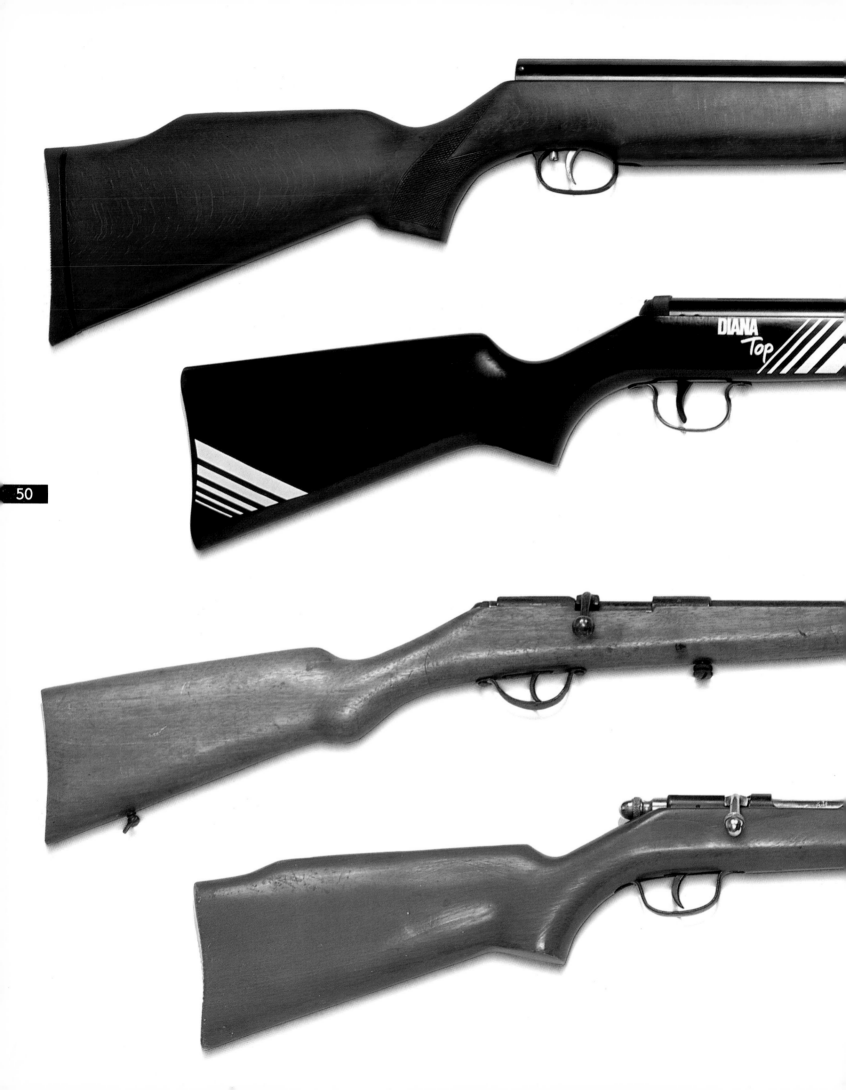

**Weihrauch, HW 80**
Caliber: 4.5mm
Weight: 4kg (8 lb 13 oz)
Overall length: 1150mm (45 in)
Barrel length: 500mm (20 in)

Single-shot rifle with drop-down, non-locking barrel. Powered by spring-compressed air. Special high-power model (253 m/sec – 830 ft/sec). Micro-click sighting system and adjustable trigger. Dovetail mounting fitted for optical sight. Stock with cheekpiece, checkered pistol grip and rubber butt plate.

**Model 28 Diana**
Caliber: 4.5mm
Weight: 3.1kg (6 lb 13 oz)
Overall length: 1090mm (43 in)
Barrel length: 440mm (17 in)

De luxe "fast-trigger" rifle. Monte Carlo stock with rubber butt plate.

# CARBINES
## AIR RIFLES

**Bolt action garden rifle**
Caliber: 12mm
Barrel length: 650mm (25.5 in)

Clearly marked with the Saint-Etienne punch. The breech body is still nicely marbled. Cranked lever. Wood sound with nice patina.

**Gaucher garden rifle**
Caliber: 9mm Flobert
Weight: 2.1kg (4 lb 10 oz)
Overall length: 1050mm (41 in)
Barrel length: 620mm (24.5 in)

Single-shot rifle, chromed breech. Frame and barrel 80 percent bronzed with tarnish along the whole of the right side.

**Manufrance, Reina model**
Detachable 8-shot magazine
Caliber: 22 LR
Weight: 2.55kg (5 lb 10 oz)
Overall length: 1060mm (41.5 in)
Barrel length: 565mm (22 in)

Nicely presented semi-automatic. Muzzle threaded to accept a sound moderator. Mounting for telescopic sight. Tangential sight with cursor.

**Humbert carbine**
Single shot
Caliber: 22 short
Barrel length: 600mm (24 in)

Manufactured just after the Second World War, excellent quality. Bolt-action breech, round barrel. Altogether superb.

# CARBINES
## THE 22

**Unique Model T Dioptra rifle**
Detachable 9-shot magazine
(5-shot in 22 magnum format)
Caliber: 22 LR
Weight: 2.9kg (6 lb 6 oz)
Overall length: 1045mm (41 in)
Barrel length: 600mm (24 in)

De luxe 22 LR weapon. Steel breech and casing. Adjustable trigger, manual safety catch locks firing-pin. Adjustable rearsight, mounting for telescopic or optical sight. Good quality walnut woodwork with plastic butt plate. Muzzle threaded to accept sound moderator.

**Anschütz 1516ST rifle**
Detachable 4-shot magazine
Caliber: 22 Magnum
Weight: 2.8kg (6 lb 3 oz)
Overall length: 1030mm (40.5 in)
Barrel length: 570mm (22.5 in)

De luxe weapon with breech bolt and helical groove cocking system. Push button side safety. Retractable rearsight and beaded tunnel frontsight. Fine walnut Monte Carlo stock with checkered pistol grip.

Winchester 94 Ranger
7 shot
Caliber: 30-30 W
Weight: 3kg (6 lb 10 oz)
Overall length: 960mm (38 in)
Barrel length: 510mm (20 in)

This is a version of the most popular Winchester rifle of all. Over six million of the 94 have been made, and it is still in production. When it started (1894) this rifle was specially designed to use the new smokeless powder ammunition.

Winchester 9422 Walnut
15 shot
Caliber: 22 LR
Weight: 2.83kg (6 lb 4 oz)
Overall length: 950mm (37 in)
Barrel length: 520mm (20.5 in)

Though the manufacturer says the Winchester 9422 is a derivative of the 94, in fact they are only alike in outward appearance. The 9422 has a different mechanism from the 94. The 9422 is side ejecting, while the 94 is top ejecting. The 9422 is available in several versions, and is still an interesting weapon.

# WESTERN RIFLES

The development of firearms in America followed the technical and industrial revolution of the 19th century which triggered the great wave of human immigration that preceded the long journey westward over the vast plains of the United States. Disdained by the armies of Europe, the new American breech-loaders equipped every immigrant, rider, adventurer, gold prospector and peddler of every kind of dream: the Spencer, the Smith, the Henry, the Springfield, the Winchester and the Remington Rolling Block.

These guns bring back memories of the wonderful Westerns of our childhood, when the good cowboys confronted the wicked rustlers and the outlaw train robbers. The epic stories of how the West was won, and of the gold rush, are conjured up for us again whenever we handle an old Winchester. For the Winchester, in all its many versions and variants, is the symbolic weapon of that age. Other manufacturers were to follow the route marked out by the firm from New Haven, Connecticut, and produced lever-loaded carbines of their own. Though these rifles had the advantage of a high-capacity tubular magazine, they were less practical to fire in the prone position.

Other famous weapons of the time include the Remington Rolling Block carbine. The Rolling Block action is simple, rugged and reliable under all conditions, so weapons of this type could fire some very powerful ammunition.

Winchester 1876 rifle, 3rd type
12 shot
Caliber: 45-60
Weight: 4.2kg (9 lb 4 oz)
Overall length: 1270mm (50 in)
Barrel length: 710mm (28 in)

Winchester 1873 musket, 3rd type
17 shot
Caliber: 44-40
Weight: 4.1kg (9 lb)
Overall length: 1250mm (49 in)
Barrel length: 760mm (30 in)

Winchester 1887 30" barrel shotgun
5 shot
Caliber: 10mm
Weight: 3.9kg (8 lb 9 oz)
Overall length: 1300mm (51 in)
Barrel length: 810mm (32 in)

Winchester 1873 24" round barrel
25 shot
Caliber: 22 short
Weight: 3.85kg (8 lb 8 oz)
Overall length: 1000mm (39.5 in)
Barrel length: 510mm (20 in)

The Winchester 1876 was created to conquer the military market. This was because the ammunition of the 1873 was not powerful enough for purely military use. It was therefore necessary to bring out a sort of super 1873. Octagonal barrel. Some 80 percent original blue, the rest paler or tobacco sheen. Part mirror-bright inside with very fine rifling and a little oxidation. Markings clearly legible. Sound, patinated woodwork. Very consistent weapon. Folding trigger.

This is the infantry musket version of the 1873. All Winchester enthusiasts think of the 1873 as "the real Winchester" or even "the king of the West." Fully rebronzed metal still showing just a trace of oxidation. Part mirror-bright inside with very fine rifling and a little oxidation. Legible markings. Stock in good condition with patina. The foregrip also has patina and slight wear. This weapon will accept a socket bayonet.

# LEVER ACTIONS
## THE OLD DAYS

This weapon, originally produced by Winchester to give it a presence in the sporting shotgun market, was issued to escorts of money shipments by the Adams Express Co for protection against train robbers. Dark gray steel frame. Magazine and barrel 50 percent blue, the rest tobacco. Clearly legible markings. Patina on woodwork, banded butt plate.

Carbine version of the 1873. White steel metalwork with tiny spots of oxidation. Sound woodwork with patina. Rare in this caliber, since only 19,738 were produced.

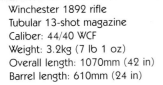

**Winchester 1892 rifle**
Tubular 13-shot magazine
Caliber: 44/40 WCF
Weight: 3.2kg (7 lb 1 oz)
Overall length: 1070mm (42 in)
Barrel length: 610mm (24 in)

The 1892 Winchester uses the 1886 pattern mechanism, but in the caliber that succeeded for the 1873 model. Octagonal barrel, tubular magazine. Metal rebronzed long ago and now clear in places. Some polishing marks and a few signs of tarnish. Mirror-bright inside, superb rifling. Markings are clearly readable on the barrel, readable on the back frame. Number poorly re-engraved by hand. Stock and forepiece restored in fine walnut.

**Savage 99 rifle**
5 shot
Caliber: 303 Sav
Weight: 3.4kg (7 lb 7 oz)
Overall length: 1010mm (40 in)
Barrel length: 550mm (21.5 in)

The American firm of Savage has been producing lever carbines since 1892. The Savage differs from other weapons of this type by not having an external hammer and having a detachable magazine. Dark gray steel with traces of oxidation on the frame. Markings clearly readable. Stock expertly restored. Front end cleaned, slightly recessed.

# LEVER ACTIONS
## THE OLD DAYS

**Spanish Tigre rifle, 1892 pattern**
5 or 11 shot
Caliber: 44/40 WCF
Weight: 3.2kg (7 lb 1 oz)
Overall length: 1000mm (39.5 in)
Barrel length: 560mm (22 in)

This is a "certified copy" of the 1892 Winchester produced by the Basque firm of Eibar G. Arate y Cia. Manufactured in the nineteen-twenties for the Central and South American market. Frame and barrel 80 percent bronzed, with oxidation bloom. Tobacco patina on the tubular magazine. Readable markings. Wood has patina and signs of handling. Weapons of this type were used in 1936 during the Spanish Civil War.

**Winchester 1892 carbine**
5 or 11 shot
Caliber: 44/40 WCF
Weight: 2.5kg (5 lb 8 oz)
Overall length: 955mm (37.5 in)
Barrel length: 510mm (20 in)

This is the carbine version of the 1892 Winchester. Metal rebronzed some time ago. Some pitting on the barrel and magazine. Clearly readable markings. Sound, patinated woodwork. The stock is not original. There is a join on the right of the grip.

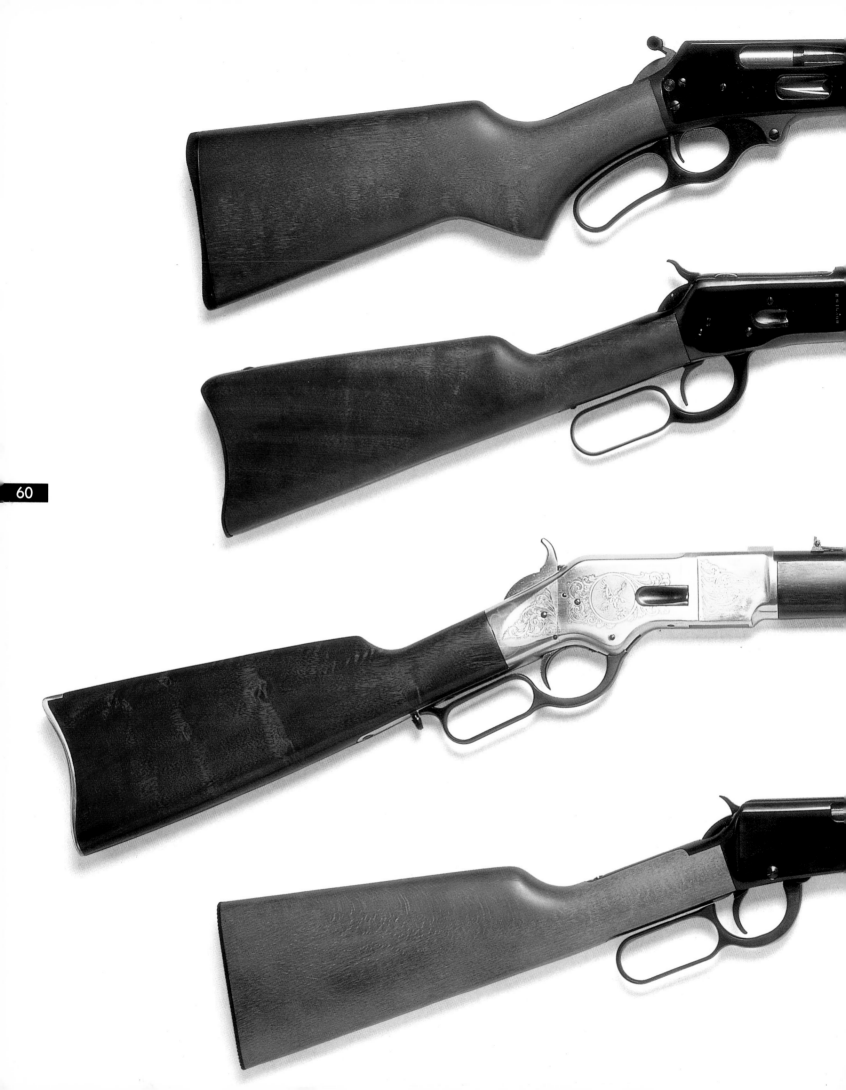

**Marlin 336 CS rifle**
5th catgory weapon
Tubular 7-shot magazine
Caliber: 30-30 Winchester
Weight: 3.18kg (7 lb)
Overall length: 970mm (38 in)
Barrel length: 510mm (20 in)

Marlin firearms have been Winchester's great competitors since 1880. The main difference between the guns of these two manufacturers lies in the direction in which they eject spent cases. Winchesters eject at the top and Marlins on the right. The advantage of side ejection as on the Marlin is that a telescopic sight can be fitted.

**Rossi Puma**
Caliber: 44 Magnum
Weight: 2.75kg (6 lb 1 oz)
Overall length: 955mm (37.5 in)
Barrel length: 508mm (20 in)

Western rifle produced by the famous Brazilian manufacturer Amadeo Rossi. This one is based on the famous 1892 Winchester. Stock and foregrip in framira (an exotic Brazilian wood) with a walnut finish.

# LEVER ACTIONS
## MODERN TIMES

**Uberti Yellow Boy**
9 shot
Caliber: 44-40 WCF
Weight: 3.35kg (7 lb 6 oz)
Overall length: 970mm (38 in)
Barrel length: 465mm (18 in)

This is a replica of the first Winchester, the famous 1866 carbine. For the record, during the Franco-Prussian War of 1870 the French government ordered three thousand 1866 Winchesters.

**Erma EG 712**
15 shot
Caliber: 22 LR
Weight: 2.4kg (5 lb 4 oz)
Overall length: 920mm (36 in)
Barrel length: 470mm (18.5 in)

This weapon from the German firm of Erma in Dachau is strongly influenced by the Winchester 9422. Rearsight can be adjusted for height, provision for mounting an optical sight. English style stock and foregrip in beech finished as walnut.

**Remington Rolling Block "Creedmoor Rifle"**
Caliber: .45-70 Government
Weight: 5.5kg (12 lb 2 oz)
Overalll length: 1405 mm (55 in)
Barrel length: 1010mm (40 in)

The weapon shown here is a modification of the original model attributed to the famous Italian manufacturer Pedersoli. The creator of this version, a gunsmith from the French town of Grenoble, has polished the breech casing, fitted a sight mounting and attached a telescopic sight. There have been some slight alterations to the woodwork. Quite magnificent.

**Remington Rolling Block "Buffalo Rifle"**
Caliber: .45-70 Government
Weight: 5.5kg (12 lb 2 oz)
Overalll length: 1390 mm (nearly 55 in)
Barrel length: 995mm (39 in)

The differences between this rifle and the previous one include a straighter stock, a shorter telescopic sight and a fractionally shorter barrel.

# ROLLING BLOCK

**Remington Rolling Block "Cavalry"**
Caliber: .45-70 Government
Weight: 3.8kg (8 lb 6 oz)
Overalll length: 1305 mm (51 in)
Barrel length: 910mm (36 in)

Cavalry version of the Rolling Block rifle.

**Remington Rolling Block for Argentina**
Caliber: .43 Spanish
Weight: 4.1kg (9 lb)
Overalll length: 1305 mm (51 in)
Barrel length: 910mm (36 in)

Marked: "E. Remington & Sons Ilion N.Y. USA." Metalwork 90% bronzed, very fine. Clearly readable markings. Woodwork cleaned and sound. The Remington Rolling Block was originally made from components for the 1863 Springfield rifle. It was very soon being made from original parts. This single-shot breech-loader had enormous international success. The French Army used it during the war of 1870. Many versions of the Remington Rolling Block were made. They differ only in caliber and overall length. In all other respects their mechanisms are identical.

Japanese matchlock arquebus
Caliber: 50
Weight: 3.86kg (8 lb 8 oz)
Overall length: 1275mm (50 in)
Barrel length: 1055mm (41.5 in)

This weapon was originally produced by a Portuguese trader who landed on the Japanese island of Tanegashima in 1543. Brass lock, dog-head and pan-cover, internal mechanism. Octagonal barrel attached to the foregrip by brass hoops.

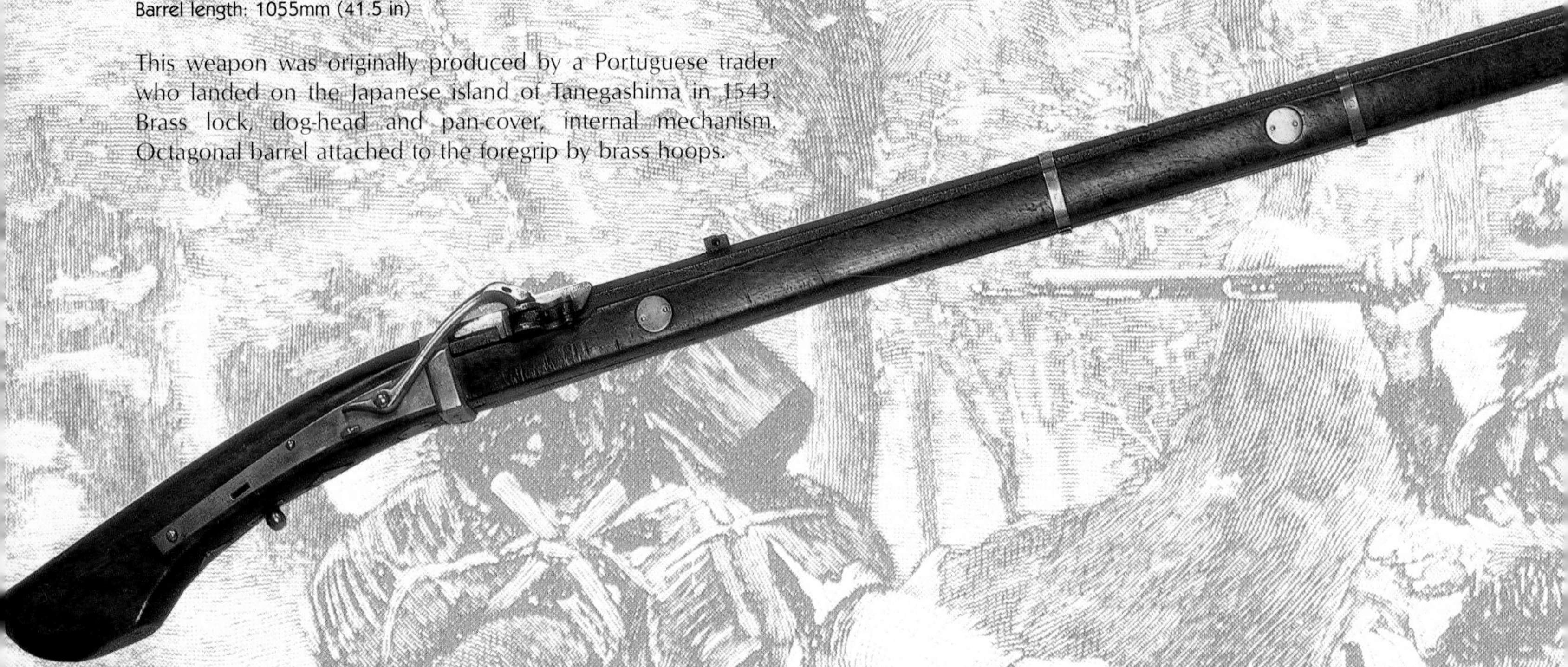

Deerhunter
Caliber: 45
Weight: 2.95kg (6 lb 8 oz)
Overall length: 1030mm (41 in)
Barrel length: 700mm (28 in)

The Deerhunter took over from the Kentucky rifle in 1812 because it was easier to use. It was immortalized by the exploits of Western hero Jeremiah Johnson during his intrepid and dangerous mission in the Rockies. Octagonal rifled barrel, mottle-finish lock, adjustable trigger, leaf-spring percussion system.

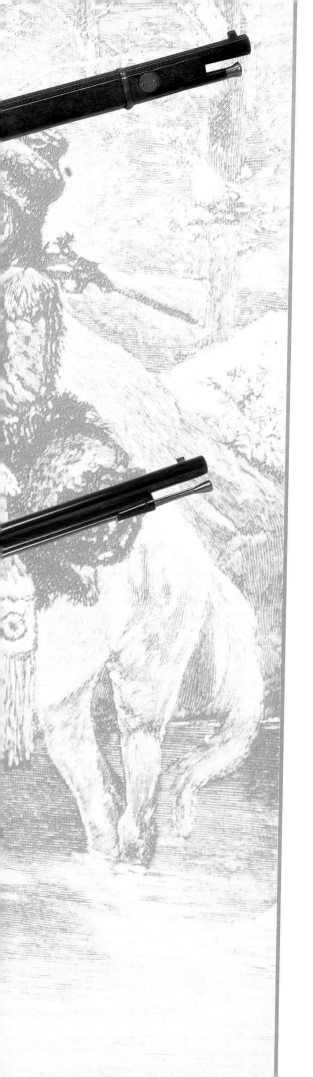

# BLACK POWDER RIFLES

Black powder rifles can be thought of as another aspect of weapon collecting. In fact it is not very advisable to shoot with a genuine antique firearm due to the ever-present risk of both injury and damage to the weapon.

The answer is to get a replica antique firearm. Its barrel will have been manufactured to modern standards and inspected on a test-bench to ensure complete safety for the shooter. With a replica there is no risk of the weapon exploding in your face.

The great specialist manufacturers of replica firearms are to be found in Italy and America.

Black powder shooting has many charms. There is the satisfaction of mastering weapons which are at once simpler in design and more complex to use than modern guns; there is the chance to see how our ancestors used to shoot; and in some places, the hunting season using black powder guns is longer than it is if you use modern weapons.

Don't run away with the idea that replica guns fire wide. On the contrary, they are highly accurate weapons that will bring you a great deal of pleasure.

Kentucky rifle
Caliber: 45
Weight: 3.3kg (7 lb 4 oz)
Overall length: 1220mm (48 in)
Barrel length: 850 (33.5 in)

The Kentucky is the most famous rifle used during the taming of the West. It was developed in Lancaster USA by gunsmiths who were mainly from German-speaking countries. The Kentucky is light but not very convenient to use, being long and not having a carrying sling.

Harper's Ferry 1803
Caliber: 54
Weight: 3.885kg (8 lb 9 oz)
Overall length: 1200mm (47 in)
Barrel length: 833mm (32.75 in)

Here is one of the very first rifle-barreled flintlock guns to become regulation issue for the United States Army. It was standard equipment for, among others, the members of the famous Lewis and Clark Expedition of 1804, sent to reconnoitre the territories to the west of the Mississippi and Missouri rivers.

# FLINTLOCKS

Scout
Caliber: 45
Weight: 3kg (6 lb 5 oz)
Overall length: 1150mm (45 in)
Barrel length: 800mm (31 in)

The Scout is actually just a shortened version of the Kentucky. It was produced to overcome the awkwardness of using the latter.

**Mountain rifle**
Caliber: 45
Weight: 3.6kg (7 lb 15 oz)
Overall length: 1200mm (47 in)
Barrel length: 800mm (31 in)

Replica of a classic hunting rifle from the time of the American pioneers. This weapon is almost identical to the Hawken 1825 model. Octagonal rifled barrel, two stop pins and German set trigger. Finely engraved on the lock and dog-head.

**Kentucky 1825 Tennessee**
Caliber: 45
Weight: 3.3kg (7 lb 4 oz)
Overall length: 1220mm (48 in)
Barrel length: 850mm (33.5 in)

Replica of the famous Kentucky rifle's conversion to percussion. The Kentucky was a favorite with American trappers and pioneers. Adjustable trigger and octagonal rifled barrel.

**Ranger rifle**
Caliber: 45
Weight: 3.2kg (7 lb 1 oz)
Overall length: 1120mm (44 in)
Barrel length: 710mm (28 in)

Spanish-made percussion rifle. Octagonal barrel. The "Buckhorn" type rearsight can be adjusted for height. Marbled locks.

**Hawken Hunter**
Caliber: 58
Weight: 4kg (8 lb 13 oz)
Overall length: 1140mm (45 in)
Barrel length: 720mm (28 in)

Replica derived from the Hawken rifle of 1825, this in turn being derived from the Kentucky rifle. The only two differences between this version and the original relate to the presence of two detachable rings, and the end of the stock, which is straight instead of hollow. The stock is also fitted with a rubber butt plate, and no such accessory existed in 1825.

Lee-Enfield No 4 rifle
10 shot
Caliber: 303
Weight: 4.11kg (9 lb 1 oz)
Overall length: 1128mm (44 in)
Barrel length: 640mm (25 in)

Metal looks good, nice markings. Fine woodwork bearing the same number. This is the British Army rifle of the Second World War.

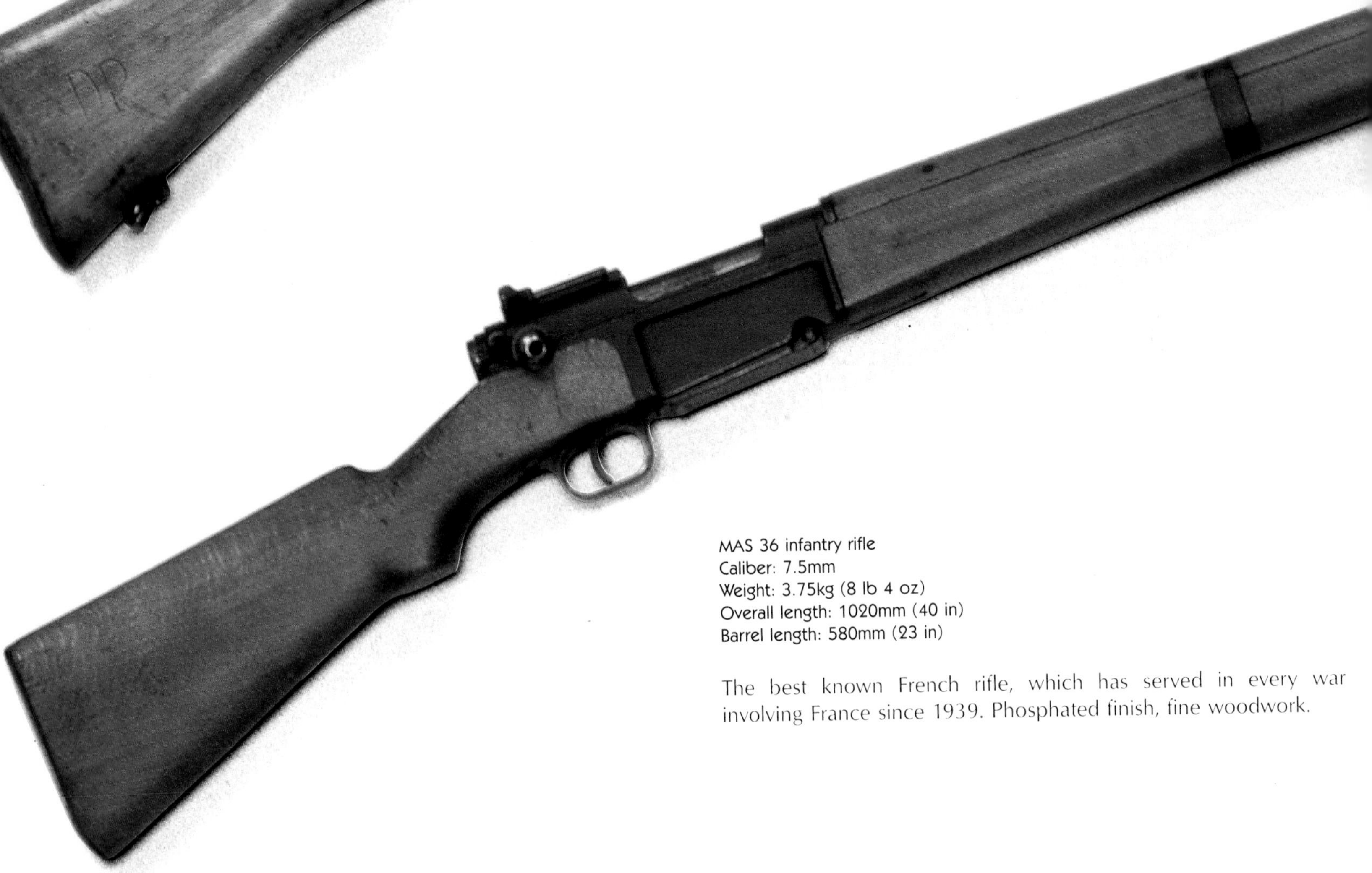

MAS 36 infantry rifle
Caliber: 7.5mm
Weight: 3.75kg (8 lb 4 oz)
Overall length: 1020mm (40 in)
Barrel length: 580mm (23 in)

The best known French rifle, which has served in every war involving France since 1939. Phosphated finish, fine woodwork.

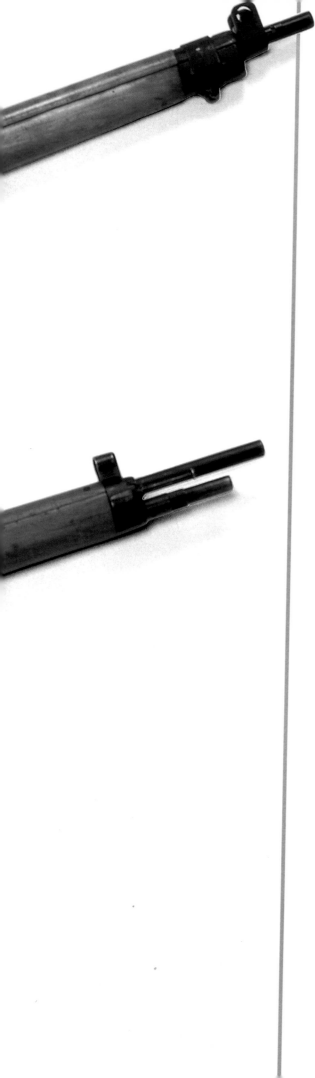

# OLD MILITARY RIFLES

Few nations could think of not manufacturing a rifle of their own, so there was a proliferation of military firearms. The rifle, the symbol of the soldier, became the symbol of nationhood. The Garand is American, just as the Lee-Enfield is British, each with its matching ammunition. Even so, weapons were imported in a good many instances.

In the 19th and early 20th centuries, rifles were either manual repeaters or semi-automatics. The semi-automatic action reloaded a new cartridge mechanically after each shot, making it possible to fire more rapidly with this type of weapon than with a repeating rifle. However, what was required at that time was not so much the volume of fire as the power of the weapon. Rifles needed to be able to hit the bull at long range. The caliber of the ammunition was therefore important. As a consequence, weapons were long and heavy but powerful and accurate. Only the cavalry had muskets and carbines, which as often as not were simply shorter and lighter versions of the regulation rifle.

Military weapons of that period may be subject to the same controls as modern military weapons, even if they are less powerful than some modern hunting guns, or they may be classified as "antiques" if the ammunition for them is no longer available.

**Lebel infantry rifle, 1886/93 model**
8 shot
Caliber: 8mm
Weight: 4.4kg (9 lb 11 oz)
Overall length: 1307mm (51.5 in)
Barrel length: 800mm (31 in)

When France adopted this firearm it was the most modern rifle in the world. Markings: "Manufacture Royale de St-Etienne" on the lock, "Modèle 1825 T" on the rear frame, "1833" on the left side. Bronzed metal, woodwork showing some handling marks.

**Japanese Arisaka type 38 rifle**
5 shot
Caliber: 6.5mm
Weight: 4.06kg (8 lb 15 oz)
Overall length: 1270mm (50 in)
Barrel length: 810mm (32 in)

This weapon was mass-produced from 1907 and remained in service until 1945. The Arisaka 38 was used in various battles in the Far Eastern theatre (Burma, Indo-China, Philippines, Thailand and so on) during the Second World War. Metal in good condition, original bronzing. Japanese markings in excellent condition. Sheet metal breech cover missing. Patina on the very sound woodwork.

# REPEATING RIFLES

**Mauser G 98 rifle**
5 shot
Caliber: 7.92mm
Weight: 4.14kg (9 lb 2 oz)
Overall length: 1255mm (49 in)
Barrel length: 740mm (29 in)

Famous First World War weapon. Made before 1918. The breech was of such good quality that it is still used today in certain modern firearms. Patina on the metalwork.

**Finnish Kivaari M 27 rifle**
5 shot
Caliber: 7.62mm
Weight: 4.43kg (9 lb 12 oz)
Overall length: 1304mm (51 in)
Barrel length: 802mm (31.5 in)

This type of firearm was used against the Soviet army during the Winter War of 1940. It derives from the Mosin Nagant. It is more rugged in design than the Soviet Mosin.

Garand
8-shot magazine
Caliber: 30 M.1
Weight: 4.1kg (9 lb)
Overall length: 1110mm (44 in)
Barrel length: 610mm (24 in)

In 1939, at a time when every army in the world was equipped with repeating rifles, only the United States had a semi-automatic rifle. The Garand, which was the first standard issue automatic rifle, saw service not only in the Second World War but also in Korea. The French Army also used it in Algeria.

MAS 49
10-shot magazine
Caliber: 7.5mm
Weight (unloaded): 3.9kg (8 lb 9 oz)
Overall length: 1075mm (42 in)
Barrel length: 580mm (23 in)

The MAS 49 is considered to be the first semi-automatic French standard issue. It had a short career, however, as it was soon replaced with an improved version that could fire modern rifle grenades, the MAS 49/56.

# SEMI-AUTOMATICS

Mauser G 43
10-shot magazine
Caliber: 7.92mm
Weight: 4.33kg (9 lb 8 oz)
Overall length: 1117mm (44 in)
Barrel length: 558mm (22 in)

Weapon much used by German sharpshooters, especially on the Eastern Front. Dark gray steel with 60 percent bronzing. The 1944 markings are clearly readable. Veneered woodwork with patina.

AK 47
30-shot magazine
Caliber: 7.62x39mm
Weight (unloaded): 4.3kg (9 lb 7 oz)
Overall length: 869mm (34 in)
Barrel length: 414mm (16 in)

The AK 47 was the second assault rifle in general service and is one of the most famous weapons in the world. It was designed in the former Soviet Union and is a symbol of freedom fighters worldwide. The AK 47 is known to be rugged, reliable, simple and highly effective.

STG 44
30-shot magazine
Caliber: 7.92mm
Weight (unloaded): 5.2kg (11 lb 7 oz)
Overall length: 930mm (36.5 in)
Barrel length: 420mm (16.6 in)

The German STG 44 is the first assault rifle in wide service. It serves as a baseline for the development of modern assault rifles.

# ASSAULT RIFLES

The assault rifle is the modern infantryman's basic weapon. The name given to this category of firearm derives from the nickname given to the first widely-used rifle of the type, the German Sturmgewehr (STG 1944). To a very great extent, assault rifles are made of modern materials such as glass fiber, aluminum and alloys. They have replaced virtually every other kind of rifle and firearm in the armies of today. The assault rifle has become something of a universal weapon. Because it is so flexible in use, it can replace many different kinds of small arms. It can be used at close range (up to 35 meters or 115 feet) or long range (up to 800 meters or about 2625 feet). It can fire single shots or bursts. It can fire rifle grenades, so giving the infantry their own pocket artillery. With the addition of a night sight such as a telescopic light intensifier (LI) it can be used just as successfully in the dark as in daylight. Its accuracy is excellent, with a better than 90 percent probability that the user will hit a target at a range of 200 meters (about 660 feet). Many assault rifles are ambidextrous. It is very compact, and can therefore be used in even the most confined spaces, such as inside armored vehicles. Because modern ammunition is so light (for instance the NATO 5.56mm or the Russian 5.45mm) the user can carry a much larger number of rounds than would have been possible with the previous generation of weapons.

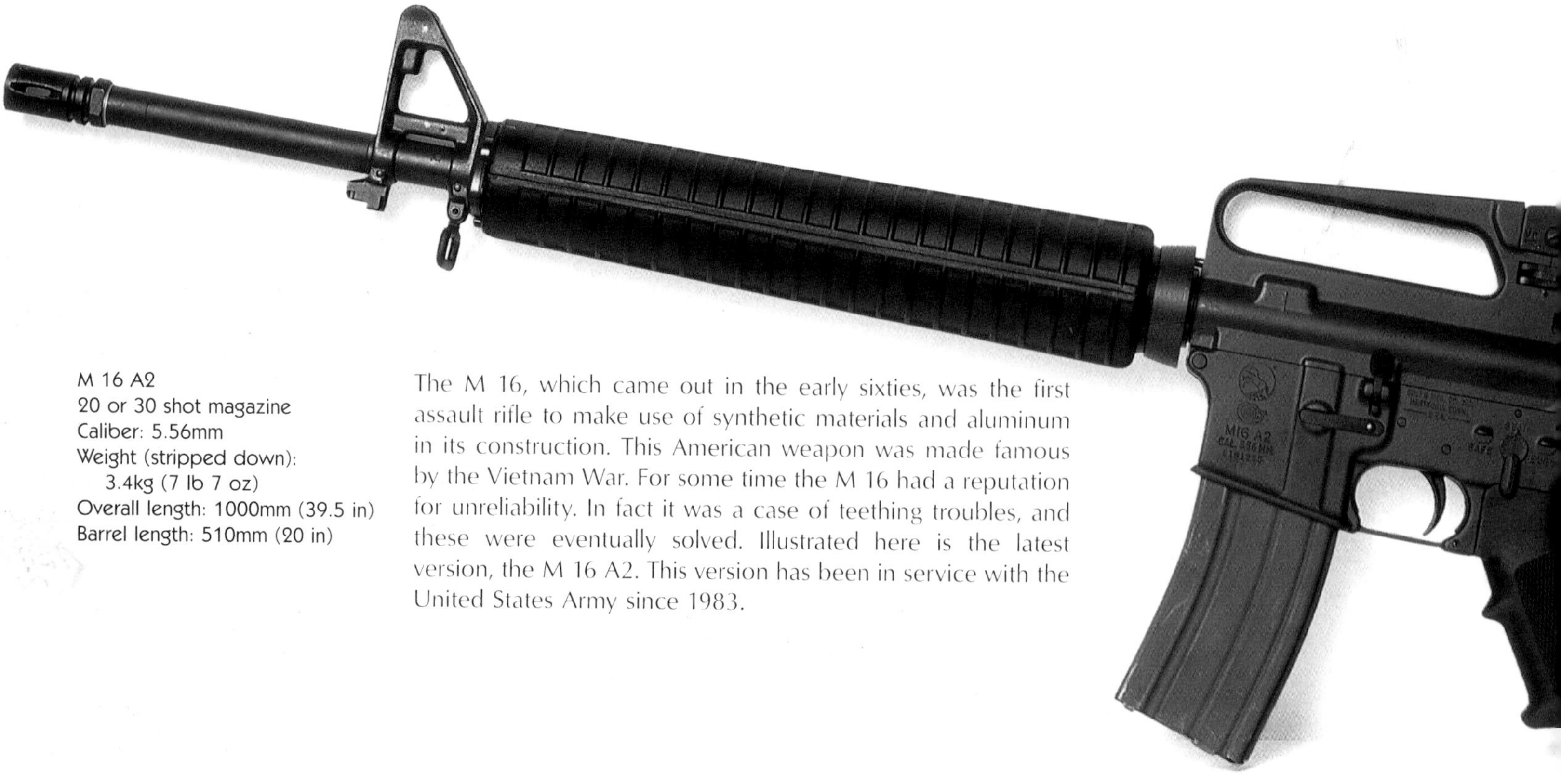

M 16 A2
20 or 30 shot magazine
Caliber: 5.56mm
Weight (stripped down):
    3.4kg (7 lb 7 oz)
Overall length: 1000mm (39.5 in)
Barrel length: 510mm (20 in)

The M 16, which came out in the early sixties, was the first assault rifle to make use of synthetic materials and aluminum in its construction. This American weapon was made famous by the Vietnam War. For some time the M 16 had a reputation for unreliability. In fact it was a case of teething troubles, and these were eventually solved. Illustrated here is the latest version, the M 16 A2. This version has been in service with the United States Army since 1983.

M 16 A2 Commando version
Caliber: 5.56mm
Weight (stripped down): 2.44kg (5 lb 6 oz)
Overall length: 760mm (30 in) with stock extended and 680mm (27 in)
with stock folded
Barrel length: 290mm (11.5 in)

The components of the M 16 A2 Commando version are interchangeable with the normal version except of course for the foregrip, which is smaller.

# THE M16

Bird's-eye view of the left side of the M 16 A2 breech casing. Above the pistol grip notice the three-position fire control selector: SAFE, SEMI = fire single shots, and BURST = fire 3-shot bursts. On the back end of the carrying handle you can see a thumb wheel for adjusting the rearsight. This was not fitted to earlier versions of the M 16 (the M 16 and M 16 A1).

AUG 77
30-shot magazine
Caliber: 5.56mm
Weight (with full magazine): 4.09kg (9 lb)
Overall length: 790mm (31 in)
Barrel length: 508mm (20 in)

AUG 77 version FM (LMG)
30 and 42 shot magazines
Caliber: 5.56mm
Weight (stripped down): 4.9kg (10 lb 12 oz)
Overall length: 900mm (35.5 in)
Barrel length: 621mm (24.5 in)

The FM (light machine gun) version of the AUG 77 has a different
barrel than the classic version. The FM barrel is longer and stouter
in order to withstand higher rates of fire. It also has an adjustable,
folding bipod for firing from the prone position. This detailed view
of the weapon shows the translucent magazine. The firer can see
how much ammunition is left. The AUG 77 has an arm-rest forward
of the pistol grip. This replaces the traditional trigger guard.

The AUG 77 (Army Universal Gewehr) is manufactured in Austria by Steyr. It is one of the most widely used assault rifles in the world. This weapon is of the "bullpup" type, that is, with the breech at the back. Part of the operating mechanism, the breech-bolt, is housed in the stock. This feature allows bullpup weapons to be smaller than so called conventional firearms like the M 16 A2. Another feature of the AUG 77 is that it has a telescopic sight as standard equipment rather than as an accessory.

This detailed view of the weapon shows the translucent magazine. The firer can see how much ammunition is left. The AUG 77 has an arm-rest forward of the pistol grip. This replaces the traditional trigger guard.

The AUG 77 is fitted at the front with a folding handle which gives the shooter better fire control and accuracy.

Galil version ARM (assault rifle light machine gun)
35 and 50 shot magazines
Caliber: 5.56mm
Weight (stripped down): 4.35kg (9 lb 9 oz)
Overall length: 979mm (38.5 in)
Barrel length: 460mm (18 in)

This is the basic version of the famous Israeli assault rifle. The Galil, heavily influenced by the famous AK 47, was created to replace the machine pistol (PM), the assault rifle (AR) and the light machine gun (LMG). The story goes that the Israelis decided to make the most of the large numbers of AK 47s they had captured in the course of their conflicts with Arab states. They developed a new assault rifle from the components of the AK 47. The new weapon was called the Galil. It had the NATO 7.62 caliber (7.62x51mm) rather than the former Soviet 7.62mm (7.62x39mm). Later, with the more general availability of 5.56mm ammunition, the Israelis produced it in the latter caliber. It should be noted that the South African Army uses a derivative of the Galil called the R4.

Forepart of the SAR. The handrest is very large.

Right side with stock folded.

Folding Galil stock fitted with a wooden cheekpiece.

Notice there are two fire control selectors. This one, located at the top of the pistol grip, is different from the selector on the right side panel, which is identical to the one on the AK 47. The Galil can also be fitted with a telescopic sight as this photograph shows. The ARM has a bipod and carrying handle.

# THE GALIL

Galil SAR (short assault rifle)
35 and 50 shot magazines
Caliber: 5.56mm
Weight (stripped down): 3.75kg (8 lb 4 oz)
Overall length: 840mm (33 in)
Barrel length: 332mm (13 in)

The SAR version of the Galil is the short version, as the name suggests. The Galil SAR is intended for commando units and special forces. The SAR also has a folding stock to keep size down to a minimum.

Left side with stock folded.

Beretta SC 70/90 (special carbine)
30-shot magazine
Caliber: 5.56mm
Weight (stripped down): 3.99kg (8 lb 12 oz)
Overall length: 986mm (38.5 in) with stock extended and 657mm (25.5 in)
with stock folded
Barrel length: 450mm (17.5 in)

The Italian Beretta assault rifle SC 70/90 is the special forces
version of the AR 70/90 assault rifle.
This weapon came into service in the Italian Army in July 1990.
It has no great innovations when compared with the
competition. It will simply be noticed that the carrying handle is
detachable. This version cannot fire rifle grenades.

FAMAS G2
20 and 30 shot magazines
Caliber: 5.56mm
Weight (unloaded): 3.61kg (7 lb 15 oz)
Overall length: 757mm (30 in)
Barrel length: 488mm (19 in)

This is the latest revision of the famous French assault rifle, the FAMAS. The G2 version of the FAMAS was developed to make use of an M 16 type magazine. The G2 is intended mainly for export. It is fitted with a trigger guard of the arm-rest type as on the AUG 77. The FAMAS G2 is an excellent, completely ambidextrous weapon that will operate perfectly in the most difficult conditions. It is a bullpup-type weapon.

THE FAMAS
THE BERETTA

Remington 700 varmint synthetic
5-shot magazine
Caliber: 22-250mm
Weight (unloaded): 3.85kg (8 lb 8 oz)
Overall length: 1110mm (44 in)
Barrel length: 610mm (24 in)

The US Army has adopted a version of this excellent weapon which it calls the M24. Varmint (vermin) shooting is a hunting discipline in the United States. This type of competition is banned in some European countries, where "varmint" weapons are used in the 300 meters discipline. The Kevlar stock will not warp in extremes of humidity and temperature, unlike wood. The gun is finished in matt black to prevent reflections. This is one of the most accurate carbines on the market.

# COMPETITION RIFLES

The popular image that tends to associate competition shooting with aggressive behavior is totally wrong.

An edgy and aggressive marksman has no chance of success in shooting. On the contrary, the sport demands calm and concentration combined with physical fitness and stamina. Firing 120 shots from the three positions – prone, kneeling and standing – with a weapon weighing some 7 kilograms (around 15 pounds) is no easy matter. The disciplines of competition shooting are many and varied. Some are Olympic events and others are not, and some are more popular on one side of the Atlantic than the other. The various shooting disciplines include, for example:

- **RIFLE SHOOTING:** smallbore standard rifle (50 meters, .22 Long Rifle, 60 shots); international smallbore free rifle (50 meters, .22 LR, 120 shots); large bore standard rifle (300 meters, caliber up to 8mm, 60 shots); international large bore free rifle (300 meters, caliber up to 8mm, 120 shots); English match (50 meters, .22 LR, 60 shots, prone position); 50 meters running-boar target (.22 LR, 60 shots); bench rest.

- **AIR RIFLE:** 10 meter rifle (4.5mm, 60 shots man, 40 shots woman, standing); 10 meters running-boar target (4.5mm, 40 shots).

- **CLAY SHOOTING:** Olympic trap, Olympic skeet, sporting.

- **OTHER DISCIPLINES:** army-rifle accuracy and speed test, biathlon, universal trap, clay pigeon, varmint, long range, sniper, practical rifle, practical shotgun, silhouette rifle.

Feinwerkbau model 300S rifle
Caliber: 4.5mm
Weight: 4.9kg (10 lb 12 oz)
Overall length: 1070mm (42 in)
Barrel length: 503mm (20 in)

Feinwerkbau model 300S Junior rifle
Caliber: 4.5mm
Weight: 4kg (8 lb 13 oz)
Overall length: 1020mm (40 in)
Barrel length: 470mm (18.5 in)

# AIR AND GAS
## 10-METER RIFLES

Basic model for air-rifle shooting competitions. Side charging lever. Adjustable trigger. No recoil due to the inclusion of a mass-damping system. Micro-click optical sighting system. The 300S Junior version differs from the basic version only in being lighter and having a shorter barrel.

Anschütz model 2001 rifle
Caliber: 4.5mm
Weight: 4.75kg (10 lb 7 oz)
Overall length: 1130mm (44.5 in)
Barrel length: 700mm (27.5 in) – 420mm rifled (16.5 in)

High-level competition rifle. Pre-compressed air, adjustable stock, light trigger, easy charging, micro-click optical sighting system with iris for back-lit targets.

# AIR AND GAS
## 10-METER RIFLES

Walther model CG90 rifle
Caliber: 4.5mm
Weight: 5kg (11 lb)
Overall length: 1120mm (44 in)
Barrel length: 480mm (19 in)
Sighting rib length: adjustable from 795 to 845mm (31 to 33 in)

High-level competition rifle operated by $CO_2$. The $CO_2$ cylinder is housed in the foregrip. Ergonomic stock with cheekpiece and adjustable butt plate. The weapon is fully ambidextrous. Barrel suspended on metal pin, adjustable trigger. Frontsight with interchangeable sighting tunnel system, prismatic and micro-adjustable optical sight with anti-glare sleeve.

Anschütz model 2013 Super Match Special rifle
Caliber: .22 LR
Weight: 7kg (15 lb 6 oz)
Overall length: 1110-1170mm (43.5-46 in)
Barrel length: 690mm (27 in) – 500mm rifled (19.5 in)

Single-shot weapon. Shoulder adjustable in every direction, trigger adjustable up to 100 grams. Walnut stock with thumb-hole and checkering. Barrel rifled for 500mm, detachable barrel sleeve. Anschütz model 7002 universal optical sight with provision for fitting telescopic system.

Anschütz model 54 rifle

As recently as ten years ago this rifle was among the top of the range, and yet it is no longer made. We show it here with the latest model in the Anschütz range to give an idea of how much technical progress has been made in this weapons category in those ten years.

# Skeet Shooting

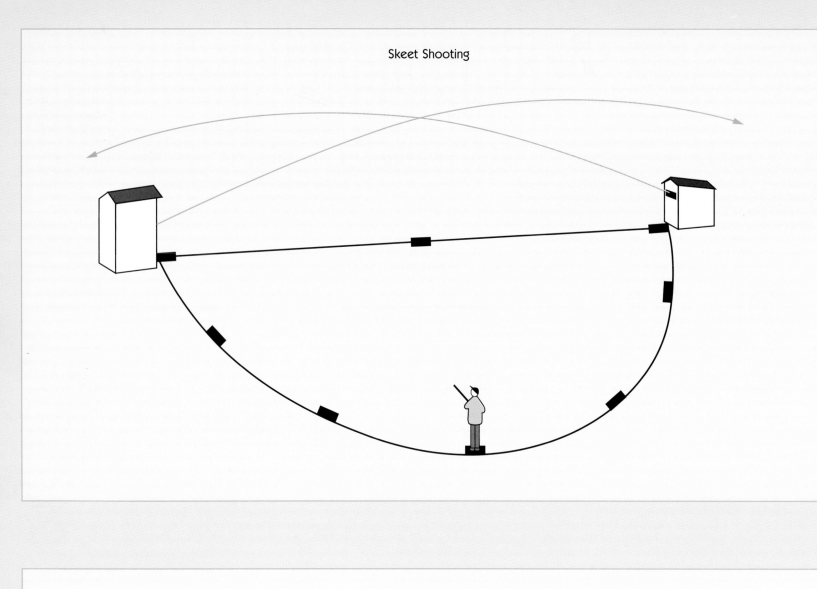

# Trap Shooting (Universal Trap)

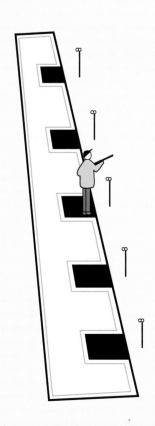
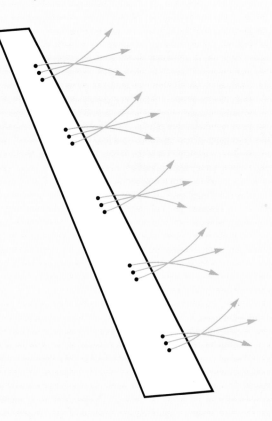

# CLAY SHOOTING

Rifle shooting, or trap shooting, made its appearance as a sport at the beginning of the 18th century. It is now accessible to all, and is being taken up by an increasing number of enthusiasts. There are three main specialties: skeet, trap and sporting.

**SKEET** is the major rifle shooting discipline. It takes place on a range that comprises two cabins called the high house and the low house. These face one another at a distance of 40 meters (some 130 feet). Flying targets (clays) are launched from these houses along consistent, predetermined paths. There are eight shooting stations on the range. Seven of them are arranged in a semi-circle between the houses. The eighth is positioned midway along the straight line joining the two houses. The shooter goes from station to station, and is not allowed to shoulder the gun until the clay has been launched. A competition involves shooting at 200 clays in groups of 25 consecutively.

For **TRAP** the shooter is positioned on a line (or trap) with five stations. Launchers are placed 15 meters (50 feet) from the line, in groups of three at five different locations. The shooter does not know the angle of flight, and shoulders the rifle before calling for launch, moving to a new station after each shot. Here too, a competitor shoots at 200 clays in groups of 25. There are two main variants: universal trap (five launchers, one per station) and American trap (one or two launchers).

**SPORTING** is an English invention which simulates all sorts of game breaking cover. It takes place on a varied range. Clays are launched singly, in pairs one after the other, or two at a time. Shooting angles are left to the ingenuity of the organisers. Clays may move toward or away from the shooter, may be ground skimming or high, and moving from the left or the right. The sporting discipline more than any other is an excellent substitute for game shooting.

Kettner R900 trap
Caliber: 12/70
Weight: 3.4kg (7 lb 7 oz)
Overall length: 1180mm (46.5 in)
Barrel length: 740mm (29 in)

Barrel with 3/4 – full chokes, 11mm sighting rib, cooling rib between the barrels, luminous red plastic frontsight, single selective trigger, ejectors. Arabesque and rose bouquet chasing. Tested to 1200 bars.

Browning B325 PC (sporting range)
Caliber: 12/70
Weight: 3.3kg (7 lb 4 oz)
Overall length: 1160mm (45.6 in)
Barrel length: 710mm (28 in)

Sporting layout version of the B325 model. Adjustable "Invector Plus" chokes. "Back Bore" barrels with bores enlarged to allow the shot to pass more freely without deformation for a more concentrated shot pattern. 13mm ventilated rib. Adjustable gold-plated trigger. Walnut stock, "tulip" shaped forend.

Steyr SPG-T with 6xZF 84 telescopic sight
10-shot magazine
Caliber: 7.62x51mm (308 Winchester)
Overall length: 1165mm (46 in)
Barrel length: 650mm (25.5 in)

Latest in a long line of Steyr weapons, the SPG rifle is available in three versions, UIT, CISM and T. This weapon is for long range shooting (over 300 meters – 990 feet). All metal parts of the weapon have been specially treated against corrosion. The barrel is of forged steel. Trigger, cheekpiece and butt plate are all adjustable. Veneered woodwork.

# LONG-RANGE
# SHOOTING

Krico bench rest rifle
Caliber: .243
Weight: 5.2kg (11 lb 7 oz)
Overall length: 1115mm (44 in)
Barrel length: 600mm (24 in)

Bench rest is a US discipline that has found its way to Europe. It consists of highly accurate shooting from a sitting position with the weapon placed on a rest. All weapons are fitted with a telescopic sight and therefore do not have metal sighting systems. Shooting distances range between 100 and 300 meters (a meter is a little over a yard). Bench rest pays attention to the tightness of the impact groups. Scores are calculated for five or ten shots. There are several sub-categories depending on weapon weight and caliber.

FRF1
10-shot magazine
Caliber: 7.5x54mm or 7.62x51mm (308 Winchester)
Weight (stripped down): 5.2kg (11 lb 7 oz)
Overall length: 1138mm (45 in)
Barrel length: 552mm (22 in)

Famous sharpshooter's rifle for the French Army. The FRF1 is one of the most effective weapons in this category.

Humbert HB 308
Caliber: 7.62 NATO

HB308P sniper's rifle developed by the Humbert company on the basis of a Ruger action and Delcour barrel. This is a very high class firearm for medium-range and long-range precision shooting.

# SNIPERS

Sniper rifles are to the firearm what Formula 1 is to the automobile. They are exceptionally accurate weapons. The first shot must hit the target regardless of weather or visibility. The maximum range of the classic sniper is 800 meters (around 2625 feet). Some snipers use heavy weaponry, such as the 12.7mm machine gun, in which case the range can be as much as 1000 meters (some 3280 feet).

Manufacturing arms for crack shots requires the use of computerized numerical control machines and exceptional materials. Every part must be faultlessly made. It has long been known that two items made by the same machine may look identical but in fact are not. One will be better than the other. Nobody knows for certain why this should be, and it cannot be predicted due to the many factors that affect a manufacturing process. When producing parts for a conventional weapon, a manufacturer can afford to be much more easily satisfied than when producing for a sniper rifle. The high cost of this type of firearm is in part due to the fact that many components have to be rejected and only the finest kept. This high quality weapon must on no account be too heavy or fragile. It is essential for the rifle to be fitted as closely as possible to the personal shape of the user. To assist in gunfitting, the weapon usually has an adjustable stock and bipod, among other things. A sniper rifle must also use the best optical sights available in order to perform consistently at its best.

SIG SSG 3000
5-shot magazine
Caliber: 7.62x51mm (308 Winchester)
Weight (with telescopic sight and empty magazine): 6.2kg (13 lb 10 oz)
Overall length: 1180mm (46.5 in)
Barrel length (without flash hider): 610mm (24 in)

Rugged and reliable weapon from the latest generation of precision-shooting rifles. Fitted with an anti-glare rib on the top of the barrel. Original equipment includes a Hensoldt 1.5-6x42 BL telescopic sight, but other scopes can be fitted.

SIG SG 550 Sniper
20 or 30 shot magazine
Caliber: 5.56mm
Weight (stripped down): 7.02kg (15 lb 7 oz)
Overall length: 1130mm (44.5 in)
Barrel length: 650mm (25.5 in)

Semi-automatic weapon developed in collaboration with the special units of the Swiss police. The SIG SG550 Sniper is based on the SG550 assault rifle. The Swiss Army has also recently taken up this weapon.

## REPEATING OR SEMI-AUTOMATIC
## SNIPER RIFLES

Sniper rifles operate in two different ways. They can be manual repeaters or semi-automatic. Repeating weapons are more accurate than semi-automatics. When they are fired there are no moving parts inside the breech casing, and therefore no unwanted vibrations to interfere with the accuracy of the shot.

Semi-automatic weapons are less accurate and more costly than repeaters but on the other hand they allow much faster rates of fire. The high cost of semi-automatics is due to the fact that the moving parts have to be machined with great precision in order to minimize the extent to which they vibrate. On the other hand it would be wrong to conclude that semi-automatic snipers fire wide. They are excellent weapons.

# POLICE
# SNIPERS

Ultima Ratio Intervention
5-shot magazine
Caliber: 7.62x51mm (308 Winchester)
Weight: 6kg (13 lb 3 oz)
Overall length: 1120mm (44 in)
Barrel length: 600mm (24 in)

The Ultima Ratio is a little marvel of accuracy. It constitutes a whole system of modular weaponry. It is very easy to change from one caliber to another simply by changing the barrel, which is the work of a few seconds.

Note the air of strength that emanates from the breech casing of the Ultima Ratio.

Ever since the rise in terrorism, sniper rifles, once the exclusive preserve of the military, have become part of the arsenal at the disposal of police forces and other anti-terrorist units. Police sniper rifles generally differ from their military counterparts in having no metal sights (sighting notch and frontsight). This is explained by the fact that a police officer does not have to scuttle about with his weapon, so there is no risk of damaging the telescopic sight. Also, a police marksman does not do any opportunist shooting, or to put it another way, does not have to hunt his quarry. He simply takes up the position assigned to him and waits for the target to present itself.

# POLICE SNIPERS

Steyr SSG-Police with silencer
5-shot magazine
Caliber: 7.62x51mm (308 Winchester)
Weight (with 6x42 telescopic sight): 4.95kg (10 lb 14 oz)
Overall length: 1135mm (44.5 in)
Barrel length: 650mm (25.5 in)

The SSG-P is made in Austria by Steyr. It is one of the most widely used sniper rifles in the world. The weapon is simple to use, accurate and economical.

M2 Sniper
Caliber: 300 W. magnum

Sniper rifle produced by the French manufacturer RAF of Saint-Etienne.

Mauser SR 93 Sniper
1st category weapon
9-shot magazine
Caliber: 7.62x51mm (308 Winchester)
Weight (stripped down): 5.9kg (12 lb 15 oz)
Overall length: 1230mm (48.5 in)
Barrel length (with flash hider/muzzle brake):
690mm (27 in)

The Mauser SR 93 is the latest German sniper rifle. It was designed to meet the requirements of the German Army, which needed a modern rifle for its marksmen.

**Galil Sniper**
25-shot magazine
Caliber: 7.62x51mm (308 Winchester)
Weight unloaded: 6.4kg (14 lb 1 oz)
Overall length (stock extended): 1112mm (44 in)
Barrel length: 508mm (20 in)
Telescopic sight: Nimrod 6x40

Sniper version of the Galil assault rifle. This weapon is semi-automatic.

The picture shows a Galil Sniper fitted with an ORT-MS4 light-intensifier sight for shooting at a target up to 350 meters away on a moonless night.

The flash hider/muzzle brake fitted to sniper rifles is not just an accessory but an essential component for fire accuracy and regularity. The grooved shapes on flash hiders are not for looks but for optimum effectiveness.

# MILITARY SNIPERS

**Mauser M86**
9-shot magazine
Caliber: 7.62x51mm (308 Winchester)
Weight (without telescopic sight): 6.2kg (13 lb 10 oz)
Overall length: 1273mm (50 in)
Barrel length: 650mm (25.5 in)

High quality sniper rifle, available with glass fiber or wooden stock and fittings. Note that there is a facility for fitting the telescopic sight with laser telemetry to determine the exact distance to the target.

Ultima Ratio Commando II
5-shot magazine
Caliber: 7.62x51mm (308 Winchester)
Weight: 5.5kg (12 lb 2 oz)
Overall length (stock extended): 980mm (38.5 in)
Barrel length: 470mm (18.5 in)

The new Ultima Ratio Commando sniper rifles for use by the military are noted for their great accuracy and compactness. A silencer can be fitted in under a minute. These are high-performance weapons.

Ultima Ratio Commando I
5-shot magazine
Caliber: 7.62x51mm (308 Winchester)
Weight: 5.5kg (12 lb 2 oz)
Overall length: 1080mm (42.5 in)
Barrel length: 550mm (21.5 in)

# PERSONAL DEFENSE WEAPONS

The classic personal defense weapon is the shotgun, called by some "the honest man's best friend." Defensive weapons are also needed by police forces and by military units responsible for specific tasks such as guard duty or perimeter defense. Security firms or private individuals may also have recourse to arms of this type.

The only differences distinguishing "police and military" versions from their "civilian" equivalents are length of barrel and magazine capacity. Civilian versions have longer barrels and smaller magazines.

Weapons of the "upgraded shotgun" type are by far the commonest in this group for a number of reasons. A defense rifle must above all be simple to use, reliable and safe. A few years ago police forces in some countries were equipped with submachine guns (SMGs). SMGs are very imprecise weapons in the hands of anyone who has not learned to use them properly. When firing a burst on an SMG there are often bullets which do not find their mark because the gun "rises" during firing, and stray bullets of course pose a threat to innocent bystanders. So in some cases it was decided to arm police with shotguns instead, because they are easier to use and less prone to produce strays.

Defensive weapons may be divided into three main groups: pump-actions (the well-known riot guns), automatics (in actual fact semi-automatics), and what might be termed "survival" weapons. Survival weapons are for people like aircraft pilots or explorers. They are often combination rifles for firing bullets and shot, usually light and compact.

Top left: IMI Timber Wolf
Bottom left: Beretta RS 201 M1

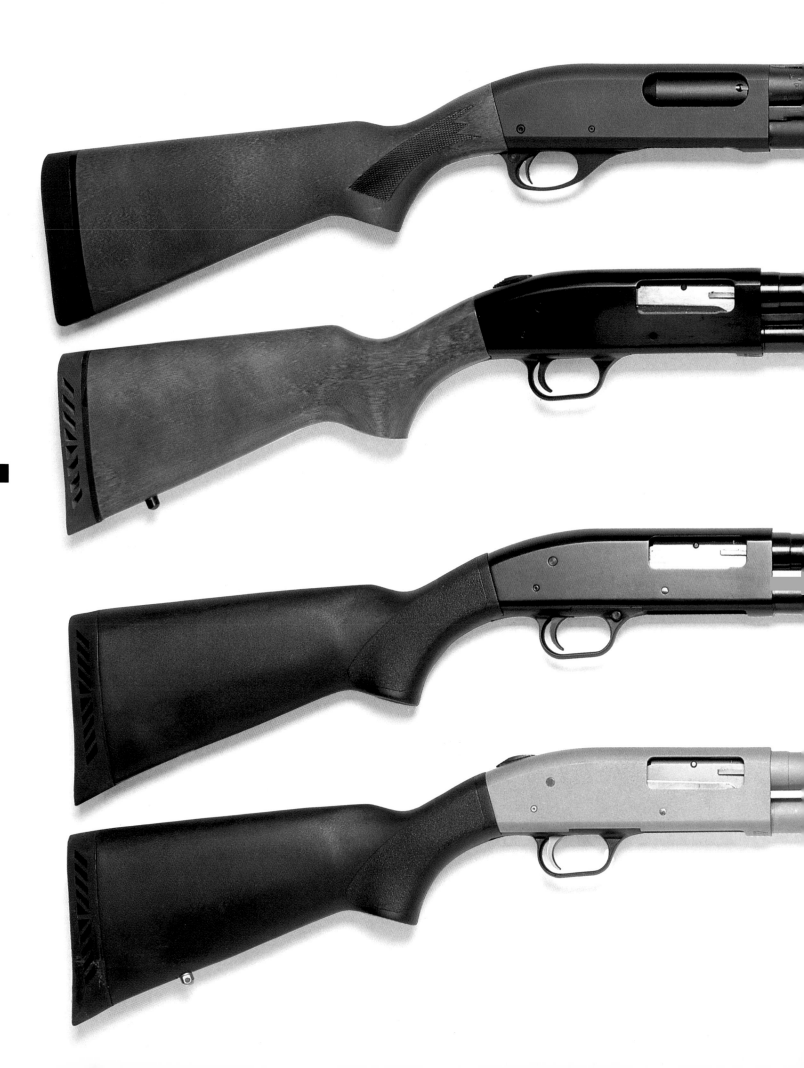

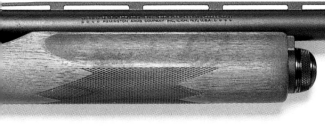

**Remington 870 Police Express**
4 + 1 shot
Caliber: 12/76
Weight: 2.8kg (6 lb 3 oz)
Overall length: 1090mm (43 in)
Barrel length: 610mm (24 in)

Multi-purpose pump-action. Ventilated rib on barrel.

**Mossberg ATP6**
5 + 1 shot
Caliber: 12/76
Weight: 3.05kg (6 lb 11 oz)
Overall length: 970mm (38 in)
Barrel length: 610mm (24 in)

Weapon from the famous 500 series produced by the no less famous American manufacturer. Light aluminum frame, black burnish. American walnut stock. Safety catches at rear and top of breech casing. No rearsight but beaded frontsight.

# RIOT GUNS

**Maverick model 88**
5 + 1 shot
Caliber: 12/76
Weight: 2.9kg (6 lb 6 oz)
Overall length: 970mm (38 in)
Barrel length: 610mm (24 in)

Very rugged pump-action gun, trigger safety, light alloy, burnished black. Synthetic stock with rubber heel plate. Barrel interchangeable with Mossbergs.

**Mossberg Mariner**
5 + 1 shot
Caliber: 12/76
Weight: 3.2kg (7 lb 1 oz)
Overall length: 970mm (38 in)
Barrel length: 610mm (24 in)

Metal parts made of Marinecote (Teflon Nickel material), which has even better corrosion resistance than stainless steel. Black synthetic stock with rubber butt plate. The firm of Mossberg, founded in 1919 by Oscar F. Mossberg, is located at New Haven, Connecticut, and is the world's largest pump-action manufacturer. The US Army is equipped with Mossberg guns, as are many police forces and special units around the world.

**Beretta 1200 F**
3 shot
Caliber: 12/70
Weight: 2.9kg (6 lb 6 oz)
Overall length: 1250mm (49 in)
Barrel length: 710mm (28 in)

Damped opening action, locked by turning the breech head. Synthetic polymer stock giving high impact resistance and all-weather performance. The 1200 FP version for security forces differs from the 1200 F in not having a sighting rib, while its barrel is 510mm (20 in) long with an adjustable rearsight. It also has a six-shot magazine.

**Benelli Super 90 M3**
6 or 7 shots depending on cartridge length + 1 in the chamber
Caliber: 12/76
Weight: 3.15kg (6 lb 15 oz)
Overall length: 1220mm (48 in)
Barrel length: 660mm (26 in)

Slug Rifle can be converted between semi-automatic and pump-action. A selector changes the operating mode as required. The breech casing is made of Ergal light alloy. Glass fiber reinforced Rislan stock, rubber butt plate. An excellent quality weapon.

# SEMI-AUTOMATICS

**Benelli M3T Super 90**
6 or 7 shots depending on cartridge length + 1 in the chamber
Caliber: 12/76
Weight: 3.55kg (7 lb 13 oz)
Overall length: 1035mm (40.5 in) with stock extended and 780mm (30.5 in) with stock folded
Barrel length: 660mm (26 in)

Folding stock variant of the previous model.

**Beretta RS202-M2**
5 + 1 shot
Caliber: 12/70
Weight: 3.85kg (8 lb 8 oz)
Overall length: 1050mm (41.5 in) with stock extended and 815mm (32 in) with stock folded
Barrel length: 520mm (20.5 in)

Basically a police weapon. Stock folds sideways, drilled sheet metal handrest, fixed sights. Muzzle threaded to take accessories such as a grenade-launcher. Matt black finish.

Sidna Commando Silencer
A version of the Sidna Commando with
    built-in silencer

Sidna mixed rifle
Caliber: .22 Hornet-20/70
Weight: 2.4kg (5 lb 4 oz)
Overall length: 1030mm (40.5 in)
Barrel length: 610mm (24 in)

Over-and-under two-shot rifle, drop-down
barrels. The upper barrel is for shot (20/70)
and the lower one for ball (.22 Hornet).

**Savage Atlas mixed**
**over-and-under**
Caliber: .22 LR-20/76
Weight: 3.62kg (7 lb 15 oz)
Overall length: 1030mm (40.5 in)
Barrel length: 610mm (24 in)

Quality weapon by the famous American manufacturer Savage. Drop-down rifle with top safety lever. External cock with selector button for changing from ball to shot. The upper barrel is for ball (.22 LR) and the lower one for shot (12/76). Ammunition and accessory stored under the heel. Detachable band swivel. Black Rynite stock. Provision for fitting a telescopic sight.

**Sidna Commando rifle**
**9 shot**
Caliber: .22 LR
Weight: 2.3kg (5 lb 1 oz)
Overall length: 950mm (37 in)
Barrel length: 500mm (19.5 in)

Manual repeating rifle, takes down into two parts at the chamber. Tunnel frontsight system, graduated rearsight can be adjusted for height. Telescopic sight mounting provision.

# SURVIVAL RIFLES

**Krico hunting rifle with SUPRA 1.5-6x42mm telescopic sight**

De luxe rifle manufactured by Krico, the great German specialists in precision weapons. The frame, rear barrel and scope mounts are superbly engraved with oak leaves. The base of the magazine is also engraved with the same design and a chamois head. The rest of the metal is 98 percent bronzed. Fixed single-notch rearsight. Double Stecher trigger. Very handsome wood with tooling at the grip and forend. A quite exceptional firearm.

# RIFLES AS ART

Whether we credit the invention of gunpowder to the Chinese, the Arabs, the Byzantines, Berthold Schwarz or the Franciscan monk Roger Bacon, it brought about the development of the first "fire-sticks," which caused more fright than damage. Refinements to firearms in the 14th century gave rise to the match-fired arquebus. In time the gunsmith became as much an artist as a technician. The rich countries of Europe took increasing delight in linking beauty with practicality, leading to a flowering of those gloriously beautiful works of art decorated with mother-of-pearl, ivory, silver, chasing and gilding.

Artistic firearms are the ultimate in weaponry. They are very often unique pieces made to order for the customer, an alliance of beauty and technical skill. The beauty comes from the choice of materials used to fashion the stock, foregrip or handrest, combined with special finishes and chasing. In most cases the chasing is in high relief, carried out by a reputable engraver who shares with the gunsmith the task of turning the weapon in his care into a work of art. Another factor that lends artistry to a gun is the quality of craftsmanship. This depends largely on the choice of steels, precision in the manufacture, convergence of the barrels and workmanship in making and assembling the action. The components are often made entirely by hand. If not they are reworked by hand in order to make highly accurate final adjustments. A weapon of this distinction is not only a joy to behold but also a delight for its user, who alone can appreciate all its qualities.

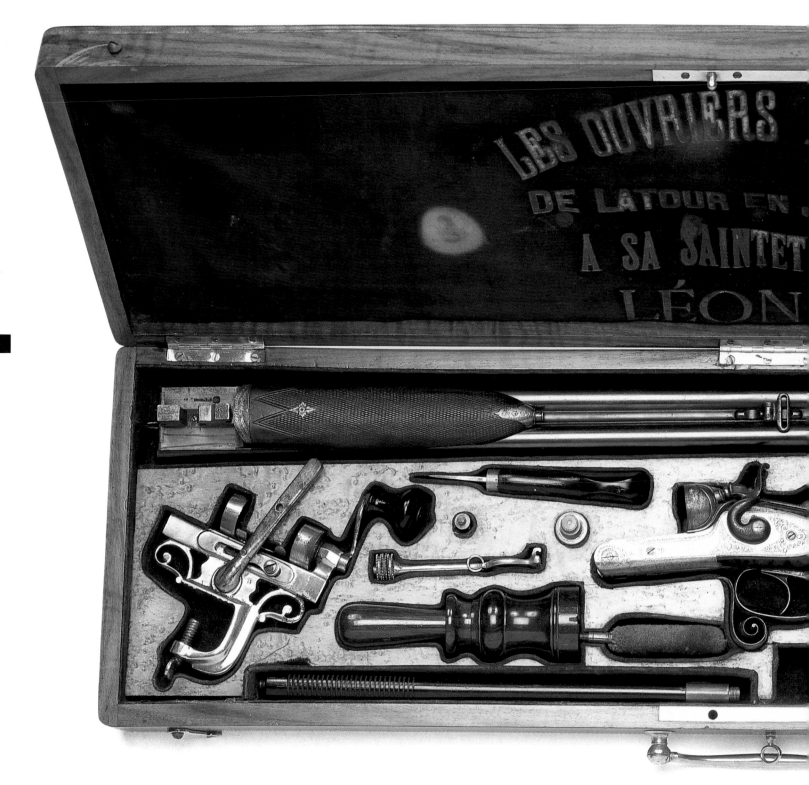

Pope Leo XIII's rifle case

Side-by-side, center-fire, .12 caliber shotgun with external hammers. Lock signed A. Rouchouse (gunsmith at Saint-Etienne, France, successor to F. Escoffier) and finely ornamented. Lovely walnut stock.

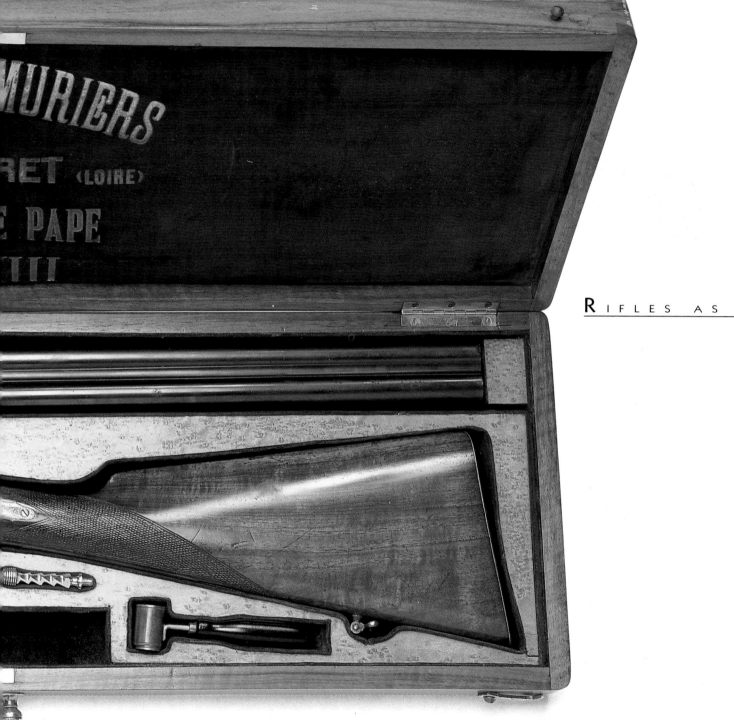

Burr walnut case with the Papal arms, velvet-lined lid inscribed in French "From the gunsmith craftsmen of La Tour-en-Jarret (Loire) to His Holiness Pope Leo XIII." Ten accessories. Presented by the Brotherhood of Christian Workers of France to Pope Leon XIII (1810-1903). Unique.

### German wheellock carbine

Weapon dated 1595, 870mm long (34 in). Superb octagonal barrel with brass punch-mark in base. The date 1595 is perfectly marked all around the punching. Gray metal with tobacco patina. Bone-inlaid cherry-wood stock engraved with mythical beasts and esoteric patterns. The stock has a split and an old join.

### Small Austrian wheellock carbine

Weapon dating from the 17th century, some 730mm (29 in) long. Gray, unornamented lock. Smallbore octagonal barrel. Delightfully decorated bronze fittings. Very fine stock with leaf-pattern moldings. Horn butt plate.

**Borovnik Jubilee Express in 9.3x74 R**

The Jubilee series was specially ordered by the firm Kettner from the great Austrian gunsmith Borovnik. Borovnik is a member of the Guild of Master Gunsmiths of Ferlach. Ferlach is a small Austrian village known throughout the world for the quality of the hunting weapons it produces. The master gunsmiths of Ferlach are known for their fine triple-barreled drillings, express rifles and combination guns. Borovnik, one of the finest craftsmen in Ferlach, is approaching retirement. The gun shown here is unique, and no more of this type will ever be made again. It is currently priced at some $40,000 (£27,000) and is expected to double in value in five years.

**Camouflaged Springfield M1**

This is a civilian version of one of the best-known American military rifles, the M 14. The "woodwork" on this version is camouflaged fiber glass. The M 14 was slightly heavy but had a reputation for accurate fire. Rare in this version.

Benelli Super 90 M3

This Benelli rifle was specially produced by the firm of Rivolier for an important Middle Eastern public figure. When compared to the original model, the external finish has been transformed and every part of the mechanism has been hand finished.

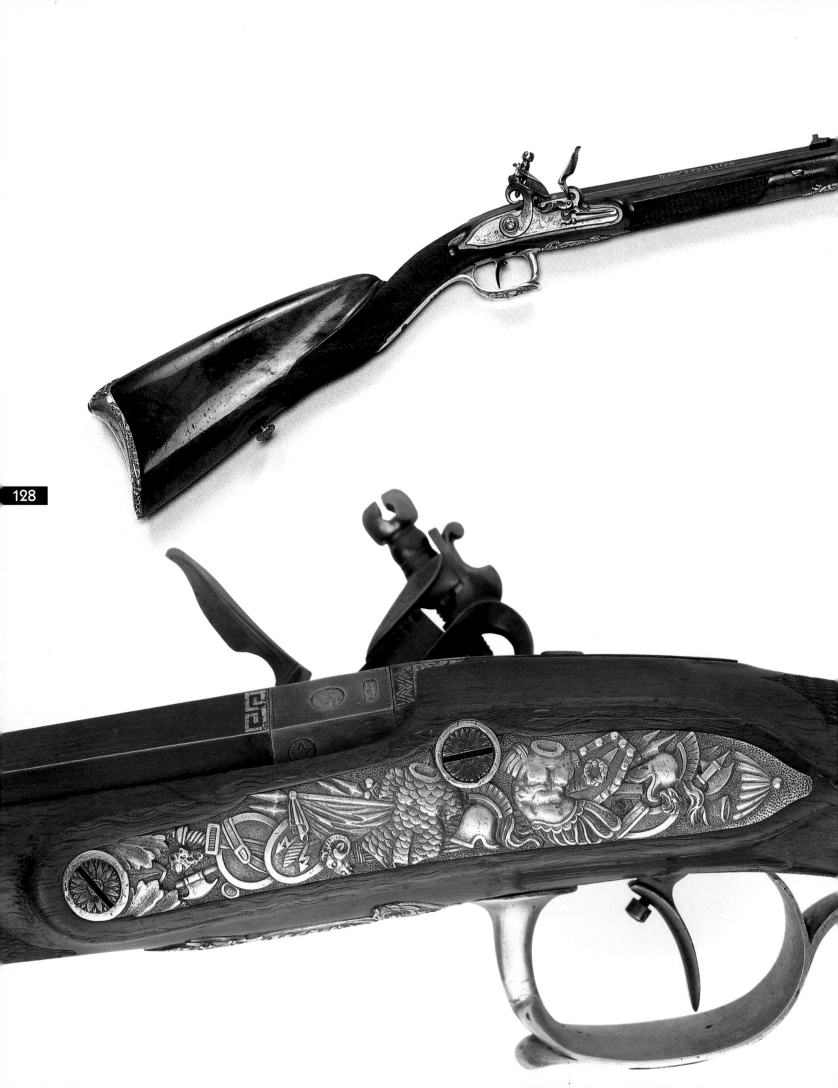

**Small rifle by Boutet**

Choice piece in remarkable condition. Superb octagonal damasked barrel marked "BOUTET ET FILS à Versailles" in silver lettering. Length: 1060mm (41.5 in). Breech inlaid with fine ornamentation and silvered punch-marks. Adjustable sights. Magnificent lock superbly engraved with imaginary beasts. All fittings are in stamped solid silver, the trophy of arms ornamentation is very deeply sculptured in the round, the whole a truly fine example of the silversmith's art. The stock is checkered at the grip and below the forend.

# ACCESSORIES

The accessories available for firearms are many and varied. In recent years many manufacturers have put more effort into producing new kinds of accessories than into developing their range of weapons. Accessories include the indispensable as well as some that are not so vital but will let you personalize your firearm according to your tastes, your needs and your pocket.

The indispensable accessories are anything to do with maintaining and carrying your gun, and include cleaning rods, solvent, oil, grease, bags, pouches, carrying cases and slings. You will also need cartridge belts. These are available in styles and prices to suit everyone.

Included among the important but not absolutely essential accessories you might consider telescopic sights. These can have fixed or variable magnification. Since variable magnification types are more difficult to manufacture, it is better to go for quality. But good quality optical sights are expensive. There are also other kinds of telescopic sight on the market, such as red dot or laser systems.

Other accessories include the bipod, which is helpful when firing from the prone position but adds to weapon weight. If you get one, make sure both its legs are adjustable. It will make all the difference on sloping ground.

Of course, there are all sorts of other accessories, ranging from ear defenders and safety goggles to rolls of adhesive tape in various colors.

# CLASSIFICATION OF WEAPONS

In many jurisdictions, the precise classification of a weapon affects the ease with which it may be legally bought, sold, kept or carried. This does not mean, however, that certain classes of weapons are banned: it simply means that obtaining a licence to buy, sell or own such weapons may be extremely difficult. Even in England, which is so often held up by pro-gun organizations as an example of the worst that can happen, it is possible (though far from easy) to obtain a license for a fully operable machine gun. It is also worth noting that where "antique" weapons may be traded freely, their exemption from firearms controls may be subject to their not being used. Even a centuries-old matchlock or wheel-lock gun may be subject to firearms controls if you load it and attempt to fire it.

What is more, there may be gaps between theory and practice. In the words of the police chief of one American jurisdiction where it is theoretically legal to carry a gun as long as it is not concealed, "If we saw you carrying a gun, we would find an excuse to stop you and ask you a few polite questions."

What follows is, therefore, only a very general guide. You should always check the law in your particular jurisdiction. It is a good idea to check with a gun club or museum before you check with the police, however, as it is not unknown for the police to make unjustified rulings based on ignorance or even on a deliberate policy of restricting firearms ownership, regardless of the actual law. In ascending order of difficulty, the various categories are as follows:

**DEACTIVATED WEAPONS** – These normally require no permits and may be freely traded. They must be rendered permanently incapable of firing, for example by welding the breech to the barrel. Even though there may be few or no controls, you still need to be careful: many jurisdictions have laws governing "imitation weapons," especially where these are used to intimidate people in the course of a crime.

**ANTIQUE WEAPONS** – Again, these normally require no permits and may be freely traded, even if they are technically capable of being fired. The definition of an "antique" is however far from clear, and if modern cased ammunition is still available for the gun, it will not normally be viewed as an antique. On the other hand, even military rifles using metallic cartridges will normally qualify as antiques if the ammunition is no longer available. As noted above, antique weapons may still be subject to firearms control if you load them. Even if there are no controls on powder and shot, you run the risk of infringing the law if you load them into a gun on which (once again) there are no restrictions.

**SHOTGUNS** – In most jurisdictions, these are subject to the least rigorous controls of any firearm, though they are every bit as dangerous as any other gun, especially at close quarters. In some jurisdictions, a shotgun license is obtainable as of right, on payment of a modest fee, provided the person requesting the license has no criminal record or other legal disability: in other jurisdictions, there are no controls at all. There may however be restrictions on the kind of shotgun that may be owned or carried. In particular, short-barreled guns and semi-automatic guns capable of rapid fire may be controlled.

**BLACK POWDER GUNS** – Whether shotguns or rifles, black powder guns are often subject to fewer controls than firearms using smokeless powder cartridges. In some United States jurisdictions, black powder guns (and the powder itself) may, however, be subject to more controls than modern weapons. This is a legacy of old, local laws that applied to black powder but which do not apply to modern weapons.

**SPORTING AND COMPETITION RIFLES** – These may or may not be subject to firearms controls, and if they are, it is normally quite easy for any law-abiding citizen to get a permit to own one. He or she may however have to demonstrate membership of a gun club, or the availability of shooting lands, or the holding of a game license. There may also be restrictions on magazine size. In the UK, special storage facilities must be approved by the police

**MILITARY RIFLES** – In general, older bolt-action military rifles are often treated in the same way as sporting and competition guns, but more modern military rifles are normally subject to more stringent restrictions. In almost all jurisdictions, any weapon that can be set for fully-automatic fire is either banned outright, or is subject to very strict licensing requirements. In many jurisdictions, semi-automatic weapons are subject to similar restrictions.

# SAFETY PRECAUTIONS

When a firearm is being transported it must always be dismantled and placed in its carrying pouch or case.

It is advisable, and sometimes compulsory, to store guns at home in a safe. This will lower the risk of accidents. Contrary to popular belief, firearms are no more dangerous than many commoner objects such as automobiles.

Most accidents involving firearms are due to carelessness or failure to observe the elementary safety rules. Here are some do's and don'ts it would be wise to follow. The list is not exhaustive.

- Keep weapons out of the reach of children.
- Never aim a firearm at anyone, even if you think it is not loaded.
- Unload your firearm as soon as you have finished using it. Point the barrel out of harm's way while you are doing this.
- Ask the owner's permission before picking up a firearm that does not belong to you, and treat it as if it is loaded.
- Do not leave your firearm unattended.
- Transport your firearms dismantled and in a lockable carrying case if possible.
- Never store arms and ammunition in the same place.
- Do not mix ammunition of different caliber together.
- Protect your hearing against noise.
- Do not assume that your weapon is safe.
- It is advisable to wear safety goggles fitted with unbreakable glass.
- On a shooting range, always follow the instructions of the session leader.
- Carry your gun documents with you to save time if there is a police inspection.
- Guns kept at home should be stored in a safe.

# USEFUL ADDRESSES –
# MUSEUMS

The majority of American museums have quite extensive firearms collections, though modern weapons since about 1950 may be disproportionately well represented. In particular, any museum with a good Civil War holding should be expected to have a wide range of weapons from that period, a time which was technically very interesting and from which many guns survive.

National Firearms Museum, Fairfax, Virginia (Closed at the time of writing, but scheduled to open in new premises in late 1994); American Police Center & Museum, 1717 South State Street, Chicago, Illinois 60603; Cody Firearms Museum, Buffalo Bill Historical Center, 720 Sheridan Avenue, Cody, WY 82414; J.M. Davis Gun Museum, Fifth & Hwy. 66, Claremore, OK 74017; Federal Bureau of Investigation, United States Department of Justice, Pennyslavia Avenue, Washington DC 20535; Gettysburg National Military Park, Gettysburg, Pennsylvania; Kentucky Military History Museum, Old State Arsenal, E. Main Street, Frankfort, Kentucky 40602; Smithsonian Institution, Washington, DC 20560; UDT/SEAL Museum, 3300 North A1A North Hutchinson Island, Fort Pierce, Florida 34949; U.S. Marine Corps Museum, and U.S. Navy Memorial Museum, Washington Navy Yard, Washington DC 20374

In Britain, the emphasis is likely to be on much older guns, though specifically military museums will have more modern weapons. The Tower of London; Imperial War Museum, London; National Army Museum, London; Victoria & Albert Museum, London; The Military Heritage Museum, Lewes, E. Sussex; National Maritime Museum, Greenwich

# BIBLIOGRAPHY

Firearms exercise a powerful fascination. There are, therefore, countless books of widely varying standards. Information on modern guns is generally harder to find than on older guns, and magazines provide the most up-to-date information as well as advertisements for the latest books. We have recommended only two books, not because there are no other good books, but because there are so many.

## BOOKS

*Gun Digest* – annual, Ken Warner, Ed., DBI Books, Northbrook IL

*Gun Digest Book of Modern Gun Values,* Jack Lewis, Ed., DBI Books, Northbrook IL

## MAGAZINES

*American Hunter,* Suite 100, 470 Spring Park Place, Herndon VA 22070

*Gun Mart,* Castle House, 97 High Street, Colchester, Essex CO1 1TH

*Guns & Ammo,* Petersen Publishing Co, 6420 Wilshire Boulevard, Los Angeles, CA 90048

*Guns & Shooting,* Aceville Publications Ltd., Castle House, 97 High Street, Colchester, Essex CO1 1TH

*Guns Magazine,* 591 Camino de la Reina, San Diego, CA 92108

*Guns Review,* Ravenhill Publishing Co. Ltd., Standard House, Bonhill Street, London EC2A 4DA

*Gun World,* 34249 Camino Capistrano Box HH, Capistrano Beach, CA 92624

*North American Hunter,* North American Hunting Club, Box 35557, Minneapolis MN 55435

*Petersen's Hunting,* Petersen's Publishing Co., 8490 Sunset Blvd, Los Angeles CA 90069

*Shooting Times & Country Magazine,* Burlington Publishing Co. Ltd., 10 Sheet Street, Windsor, Berks SL4 1BG

*Sporting Clays,* 5211 S. Washington Avenue, Titusville FL 32780

*Sporting Gun,* EMAP Pursuit Publishing Ltd., Bretton Court, Bretton, Peterborough PE3 8DZ

# ALPHABETICAL INDEX OF THE WEAPONS ILLUSTRATED

# ACKNOWLEDGEMENTS

We wish to thank the following organizations for placing the arms illustrated in this book at our disposal:

AKAH FRANCE
GIAT Industries
HUMBERT
KETTNER FRANCE
LE HUSSARD
MAUSER
PGM PRECISION
RAF
RIVOLIER S.A.
SAMSON EUROPE
UNIVERSAL ARMS

# PICTURE CREDITS

All photographs in this book are by Matthieu Prier.